THE COMPLETE ILLUSTRATED GUIDE TO FENG SHUI SECRETS:

SUPERCHARGE WEALTH, CAREER & SUCCESS WITH 87 EASY AND PROVEN TECHNIQUES

DOMINIQUE CAI

Copyright © 2021 NINE PALACES WEALTH GEOMANCY CENTRE. All Rights Reserved.

All intellectual property rights including copyright in relation to this book, The Complete Illustrated Guide To Feng Shui Secrets: Supercharge Wealth, Career & Success With 87 Easy and Proven Techniques, belongs to, NINE PALACES WEALTH GEOMANCY CENTRE. No part of this book may be copied, used, subsumed, or exploited in fact, field of thought or general idea, by any other authors or persons, or be stored in a retrieval system, transmitted or reproduced in any way, including but not limited to digital copying and printing in any form whatsoever worldwide without the prior agreement and written permission of the copyright owner. Permission to use the content of this book or any part thereof must be obtained from the copyright owner. For more details, please contact:

NINE PALACES WEALTH GEOMANCY CENTRE (52844362C)
Address: 1 Gateway Drive, #07-01, Westgate Tower, Singapore 608531
Email: enquiry@ninewp.com
Website: www.ninewp.com

DISCLAIMER: The author, copyright owner, and the publishers respectively have made their best efforts to produce this high quality, informative and helpful book. They have verified the technical accuracy of the information and contents of this book. However, the information contained in this book cannot replace or substitute for the services of trained professionals in any field, including, but not limited to, mental, financial, medical, psychological, or legal fields. They do not offer any professional, personal, medical, financial or legal advice and none of the information contained in the book should be confused as such advice. Any information pertaining to the events, occurrences, dates and other details relating to the person or persons, dead or alive, and to the companies have been verified to the best of their abilities based on information obtained or extracted from various websites, newspaper clippings and other public media. However, they make no representation or warranties of any kind with regard to the contents of this book and accept no liability of any kind for any losses or damages caused or alleged to be caused directly or indirectly from using the information contained herein.

Table of Content

Preface 10

Chapter 1: Introduction To Feng Shui and Chi 15

    What is Feng Shui? 16

    What is Chi (气)? 18

    What are External and Internal Landforms? 20

    Is Focusing on Landforms Sufficient? 22

Chapter 2: Feng Shui Techniques for Kitchen 24

    Technique #1 – Kitchen Stove and Sink 26

    Technique #2 – Beams Above Kitchen Stove 28

    Technique #3 – Size of Kitchen Entrance 30

    Technique #4 - Layout of Kitchen 32

    Technique #5 - Natural Light in Kitchen 34

    Technique #6 - Sturdy Wall Behind Stove 36

    Technique #7 - Location of Kitchen 38

    Technique #8 - Kitchen Stove And Door 40

    Technique #9 - Kitchen Equipment Placement 42

    Technique #10 - Toilet Above Kitchen Stove 44

    Technique #11 - Kitchen Stove on Island 46

    Technique #12 - Golden Triangle Formation of Kitchen 48

    Technique #13 - Kitchen Behind Deity Altar 50

Technique #14 - Open Concept Kitchen 52

Technique #15 - Kitchen and Bedroom Door 54

Technique #16 - Hidden Kitchen From Main Door 56

Technique #17 - Keeping Kitchen Clean and Tidy 58

Technique #18 - Direct Sunlight on Kitchen Stove 60

Technique #19 - Position Level of Kitchen Stove 62

Technique #20 - Kitchen Stove Sandwiched Between Water Objects 64

Chapter 3: Feng Shui Techniques for Living Room 66

Technique #21 - Living Room at Front of House 68

Technique #22 - Sofa Positioning 70

Technique #23 - Avoid Low Ceiling 72

Technique #24 - Carpet for Feng Shui Improvement 74

Technique #25 - Carpet with Auspicious Colour and Pattern 76

Technique #26 - Identifying Wealth Position 78

Technique #27 - Keeping Windows Open 80

Technique #28 - A Bright Living Room 82

Technique #29 - Walkway Behind Sofa 84

Technique #30 - Fireplace in Living Room 86

Technique #31 - Sofa Under Beams 88

Technique #32 - Ceiling and Flooring Relationship 90

Technique #33 - Cluttering Accumulates Negative Chi 92

Technique #34 - Pillar in Living Room.. 94

Technique #35 - Placement of Huge Live Plants 96

Furnitures Arrangement.. 98

Technique #36 - Suitable Furniture Size 99

Technique #37 - Making Spaces 101

Auspicious Painting in Living Room 103

Technique #38 - Avoid Painting with Weapons or Firearms 104

Technique #39 - Auspicious Painting with Nine Koi Fishes 105

Technique #40 - Auspicious Painting with Dragon and Phoenix... 107

Chapter 4: Feng Shui Techniques for Bedroom 109

Door Facing Bed.. 111

Technique #41 - Bedroom Door Facing Bed 112

Technique #42 - Toilet Door Facing Bed.. 113

Technique #43 - Avoid Poison Arrow Chi.. 114

Technique #44 - Declutter The Bedroom 116

Technique #45 - Space Under Bed 118

Technique #46 - Avoid Large Exposed Mirrors............................... 120

Technique #47 - Bedroom Door Facing Door.................................. 122

Technique #48 - Bedroom Door Facing Sharp Edges 124

Technique #49 - Bed Under Low Ceiling 126

Technique #50 - Shape of Room 128

Technique #51 - Avoid Water Feature 130

Technique #52 - Getting a Headboard for Bed 132

Technique #53 - Avoid Bed Under Window 134

Technique #54 - Avoid Fixtures Above Bed 136

Technique #55 - Underground Basement Bedroom 138

Technique #56 - Bed Above Kitchen Stove 140

Technique #57 - Plants in Bedroom 142

Technique #58 - Work Space Separated From Bedroom 144

Chapter 5: Feng Shui Techniques for Home Office 146

Technique #59 - Work Desk and Room Door 148

Technique #60 - Structural Beams Over Work Desk 150

Technique #61 - Bright and Illuminated Home Office 152

Technique #62 - Shape of Home Office Room 154

Technique #63 - Avoid Windowless Room 156

Technique #64 - Seating with Good Support 158

Technique #65 - Poison Arrow Chi in Home Office 160

Technique #66 - Celestial Animal Work Area Formation 162

Technique #67 - Spacious Area Infront Work Desk 164

Technique #68 - Avoid Back Facing Window 166

Technique #69 - Shape of Work Desk 168

Chapter 6: Feng Shui Techniques for Door 170

Technique #70 - Size of Main Door 172

Technique #71 - The External Bright Hall (External Environment) 174

Technique #72 - Long Winding Road Formation (External Environment) 176

Technique #73 - Reverse Bow Formation (External Environment) .... 178`

Technique #74 - Sharp Sha Formation (External Environment) 180

Technique #75 - T-Junction Formation (External Environment) ... 182

Technique #76 - Knife in Sky Formation (External Environment) 184

Technique #77 - Main Entrance Facing Slope (External Environment) 186

Technique #78 - Bright, Clean and Uncluttered Entrance (External Environment) 188

Technique #79 - Pillar Structure at Main Entrance (External Environment) 190

Technique #80 - Door Facing Dead-End Road (External Environment) 192

Technique #81 - Door-Facing-Door Formation (External Environment) 194

Technique #82 - Door Facing Lift (External Environment) 196

Technique #83 - Door Facing Staircase (External Environment) .. 198

Technique #84 - Door Facing Exit (Internal Environment) 200

Technique #85 - The Internal Bright Hall (Internal Environment) 202

Technique #86 - Door Facing Wall (Internal Environment)..........204

Technique #87 - Door Facing Mirror (Internal Environment).......206

About The Author..208

Preface

Feng Shui has often been a very misunderstood subject throughout time. It is often viewed as a superstition method that exists purely out of imagination to remedy life. Due to its mystical nature that revolves around Chi energy, an energy field invisible to the human eye, it is frequently exploited by unethical fraudsters promising magical remedies to ordinary folks.

With the increase of social media activity and ease of access to online content in recent times, more people are getting interested in knowing what the real Feng Shui is all about. Nevertheless, many are also daunted by this ancient metaphysical wisdom and knowledge datable as far back as 3,500 years ago.

I understand the conundrum of this group of Feng Shui enthusiasts. Despite their interest in pursuing the subject, Feng Shui is not a simple topic that can be easily mastered by reading books or online courses. The difficulty in applying the acquired theoretical knowledge in the actual environment is usually a harsh reality.

I often encountered students from around the world lamenting the difficulty of correctly applying the correct technique to the actual environment. Their learning module is usually a mixture of foundational Feng Shui studies and advanced level materials covered hastily in a few days. Many are confused by the technical difficulties but are assured by their instructors that they are competent enough to perform their assessment.

This often caused them to obtain inaccurate readings, which eventually created inconsistency in their results. Many are dismayed and disappointed, and some even accuse Feng Shui as a phony subject. I feel sorry for their learning experience and even angered by their instructors' negligent attitude towards these students' progress. I told them it is important and essential to possess strong foundational knowledge in Feng Shui principles before proceeding to the advanced level of Feng Shui studies. And this process takes longer than just a few days of studying and practice. It is a subject that took us years to master, even under the constant guidance of a trained practitioner.

However, I believe not everyone holding on to this book wishes to possess mastery in Feng Shui. Many are Feng Shui believers that want to deploy some simple yet effective technique on their place to improve their life. This book is written for this purpose because homeowners can immediately enhance the Feng Shui energy without touching on sophisticated methodology by following the straightforward landform solutions here.

I have excluded advanced Feng Shui theories, calculation, directional, or house that are deemed difficult for beginners to comprehend in this book. These topics deserved a book of their own due to their complexity, and they will be covered in my upcoming Feng Shui books series.

Feng Shui is a sophisticated topic that needs layers of foundational studies and real-life experience to obtain a certain level of mastery.

Adapting the wrong solution to a house can result in an undesirable outcome for homeowners.

This book is very much based on foundational basics that focus on observation techniques in the surrounding environment. The solutions covered are purely Feng Shui internal landforms of a house that affect the state of Chi energy through observation of the internal environment. The methods used here may seem straightforward and simple, but the effects are astoundingly accurate. This book aims to provide a simple yet effective Feng Shui methodology to help anyone achieve more incredible wealth, harmonious relationships, and more success in life.

The techniques taught in this book are a culmination of my decade-long experience in this industry from thousands of house/office/factories consultation audits conducted with my clients from many parts of the world. Many were also crystallized from my workings with property developers, architects, and interior designers that allow me to verify the consistency of various Feng Shui methodologies in larger-scale projects over the years. These are not mere theoretical teachings adapted from ancient classical manuals. All of them have been verified by my dealings with clients and other industry experts in the metaphysical world.

It is my wish for anyone reading this book to apply their newfound knowledge and enjoy the potency of Feng Shui with the result of a healthier body, fulfilling career, and happier life. The depth of Feng Shui is far and wide, and this book is perfect for giving you the right start. Constantly upscale your residential space with better auspicious Chi energy as you progress with the studies can propel you to a higher level of success.

Stay tuned to my upcoming books where I share with you my knowledge and experience, all unreserved.

Check my social media pages (http://www.linktr.ee/ninewealthpalace) for my updated content that is equally beneficial to you.

Till my next book, see you soon!

Warmest Regards,

Dom.C

Dominique Cai
March 2021

Chapter 1:
Introduction To Feng Shui and Chi

What is Feng Shui?

Feng Shui is the art of living in harmony with the environment to derive the utmost benefits of a prosperous and harmonious life by being in perfect equilibrium with nature.

To put it more visually, Feng Shui implies Wind (风) and Water (水). These are natural phenomena in nature that can positively or negatively affect the energy field of one location. When one understands the concept of a metaphysical energy field and applies the primary understanding of Feng Shui theories to these natural landscapes, the essence of benefits can be extracted and collected to affect those living or working in the area positively.

A house that complies with Feng Shui principles and abides by the required environmental forms will bring its homeowners wealth, serenity, happiness, and prosperity. The study of Feng Shui philosophy, therefore, focuses on understanding how we can choose locations from the external landscape that grants us these unfair advantages in life.

This, in essence, is what we Feng Shui enthusiasts seek in a quest to find a house that fits these Feng Shui principles.

Feng Shui principles are derived from ancient classical manuals written more than 3500 years ago. These principles are not merely philosophies written to reflect on a personal view of such a topic. They are testaments of metaphysical knowledge and wisdom refined by generations of renowned Feng Shui strategists who stood the test of time.

Based on Feng Shui classics, the study of Feng Shui fundamentally focuses on the state of Chi (氣) energy that gathers on a premise. When a house resides in an area that conforms to the Feng Shui principle of external landscape and internal landforms, the Chi energy of the residential premise is positive and desirable. And this energy enhances those living in the compound with a better state of living qualities.

Many Feng Shui principles may seem complicated and difficult to grasp in the ancient text, but they are all commonsensical theories once the reader understands its fundamentals. The difficulty lies in visualizing the state of Chi energy in an area affected by the wide variety of external and internal landforms.

Memorizing all the different states of forms with their equivalent state of Chi energy is not likely viable, as every actual landform might have a slight difference from its studied example. In order to use Feng Shui correctly and effectively, the fundamental concept of Chi energy needs to be understood right from the start.

What is Chi (氣)?

Chi is a gust of mystical energy that is present everywhere that we live. Like the air we breathe, Chi energy is intangible, colorless, and formless, and its presence can be found in every part of the world that human beings exist.

Permeating in every environmental area on Earth, Chi energy is also known as Cosmic Chi, or Dragon's Breath, which is believed to be the elixir of life governing every living human's way of thinking, behavior, and quality of life.

A good analogy of Chi energy is akin to liquid blood flowing inside of a human body. Every human organ is a divine creation capable of performing rigorous functions without rest to support our life system. However, no matter how great they are, in the absence of blood carrying oxygen throughout the many blood vessels of our body, it is just an empty shell of lifeless body parts. Blood is the essential fuel that brings the entire body mechanism to life and kicking.

The house one lives in can also be compared in this same way. Regardless of how expensive, spacious, or beautiful an apartment is, a residence without Chi energy lacks 'blood' in its premises. Whether one is living in a $3 million urban bungalow or a $300,000 rural apartment, the principles of Chi energy remain the same.

A premise that possesses stagnant or negative Chi energy can give homeowners an array of problems. They can be issues relating to wealth, health, relationship, career, family, and other life categories. Conversely, a place with positive and auspicious Chi energy flowing within can largely benefit homeowners with enhanced luck in the same areas.

Therefore, the big question lies in how to find a house that possesses positive Chi energy?

A house that abides by the Feng Shui principles of external and internal landforms is the key criteria in ensuring so.

Therefore this book is very much dedicated and focused on the internal landscape and arrangement of the house. Follow and adhere to all the mentioned pointers in this book, and the residential place should be brimming with positive Chi energy.

What are External and Internal Landforms?

External landforms are the environmental landscape configuration found on the external premise of an apartment. It can be the shapes of mountains, the size of the river, the design of buildings, or the contour of roads that form up the entire external landform.

Every individual landform needs to be considered and analyzed in detail to understand its relationship with the house façade. A good external landform can steer the environmental Chi energy to the house, making it auspicious and prosperous for anyone living on the property. This is a vital aspect of Feng Shui studies, and a considerable emphasis is based on the techniques and methods used to identify good external landform designs.

Internal landforms are the internal configuration of the house layout and design. It can comprise an individual room layout, structural design of the house, location of the door, placement of furniture, etc. Every individual arrangement and layout can affect the state of Chi energy flowing within the house premise. This is an important consideration as every change in the internal landscape that alters the flow of Chi energy can almost immediately affect people living within.

There comes the question of if a place abides by Feng Shui landform principles and is filled with positive Chi energy, does everyone living in the property enjoy the equivalent luck and benefits?

The answer is no. Not everyone living in the house gets the same pie because family members stay in different apartment rooms most of the time. The fundamental fact is that not every part of a property receives the same positive Chi energy throughout, and everyone reacts differently to a particular property segment. Some segments of the apartment may receive better quality' Chi energy than the rest. This is solely determined by the 'star positions' within the property, affecting Chi energy quality.

For an advanced Feng Shui analysis of a premise, methodologies such as Eight Mansions (八宅) and Xuan Kong Flying Stars (玄空飛星) are used for calculating 'star positions' of an apartment. These formula-based systems provide an exact position within the property that tells us which area is best for usage and which part is best to be avoided.

These formula-based systems provide a good analysis of foretelling which part of the property is best reserved for bedroom uses or which area of the land is best to be allocated for kitchen space. It also advises whether the entire house is suitable for homeowners to reside to enhance the family members' wealth, career, health, and relationship luck.

The usage of such a system is complicated and requires a more comprehensive level of fundamentals before anyone can accurately conduct its own analysis. As this book is designed for introductory level Feng Shui enthusiasts that focus on observing the surroundings rather than complex calculations, details of such a system will be covered in my next book to prevent any unnecessary confusion.

Is Focusing on Landforms Sufficient?

We know by now that the key concept of determining whether a premise is suitable for staying lies in the area's state of Chi energy. The more positive and auspicious the Chi energy is, the more convenient it is for homestayers to extract benefits from this location.

And knowing the state of Chi energy at any point in time is highly dependable on two different techniques; knowledge of External and Internal landforms and the calculation of 'stars position' using advanced calculation methodology.

Therefore, by relying solely on landform knowledge to foretell the state of Chi energy without using advanced calculation methods like Eight Mansions (八宅) and Xuan Kong Flying Stars (玄空飛星), it is only half of the analysis work completed.

However, in my opinion, this is the better option for those newly acquainted with the study of Feng Shui.

In my experience of engaging students for the last decade, students always get confused in the advance calculation segment. And most often than not, their newfound knowledge of the calculation method often resulted in the wrong analysis and solution for their house. It is incredibly heartbreaking to know some have wrongly altered their place façade based on these inaccurate analyses, resulting in a worse state than the original condition of their house.

Because the topic of Feng Shui is a complicated study, and if the user conducting audit analysis has a weak understanding of its fundamental principles, the solutions generated are often inaccurate and baseless. There have been fair shares of criticism about Feng Shui being ineffective in solving life problems, but that is primarily due to users conjuring solutions without a solid understanding of the landscape and surrounding environment.

Readers of this book should familiarize themselves with the landform techniques before ascending to the more technical-based methods. This can help them to avoid miscalculations pitfalls that may do significant damage to their property's Feng Shui.

By adhering to the majority internal landform principle of this book, any house can be at its prime to collect and accept positive and auspicious Chi energy from the external environment. Solely focusing on the landforms technique <u>is sufficient</u> at ensuring the house is brimming with positive Chi energy.

Chapter 2:
Feng Shui Techniques for Kitchen

From Feng Shui philosophy, kitchen space is a significant part of the residential home. Daily meals for the entire household are prepared in this area, and food is considered a symbol of prosperity from ancient Chinese beliefs. Therefore a poor Feng Shui design in a kitchen compound can hugely affect a family's livelihood and induce wealth-related problems. Circulation of Chi energy should be smooth and undisrupted to achieve the benefits from a good Feng Shui layout.

In addition, homeowners should pay attention to its orientation pattern and decorative arrangement conducive to the classical Feng Shui theory. The kitchen utilizes both Fire and Water elements in the Five Elements Cycle (五行) as designated for cooking, washing, and food preparation. The choices and placement of kitchen utensils, decorations, lighting, and color should be in line with geomancy principles to avoid any clash of fundamental elements.

Technique #1 – Kitchen Stove and Sink

The kitchen stove and sink are considered the most critical parts within the entire kitchen, representing Fire and Water elements of the Five Elements Cycle, respectively. Their significance is closely associated with the livelihood and wealth status of the household members. Therefore, homeowners should carefully choose their positions to create harmony and avoid any unnecessary clashes between these two elements.

When considering their positioning in the kitchen space, they should never be located directly opposite or beside each other. Fire and Water elements are not known to coexist together and are best kept apart due to their fundamental difference in characteristics. If this arrangement ensues, homeowners' health can be seriously affected, especially for the female members of the family.

Ensure the distance between the position of the stove and sink has a clearance space of at least 50 cm between them. This gap prevents Fire and Water elements from actively clashing in an undesirable kitchen layout. If the required space is narrower than 50cm, place a green plant in between them. Green plant signifies Wood element, it prevents any unwanted clashes and creates a Productive Cycle in the Five Elements Cycle by allowing Water to produce Wood, and Wood boosting Fire.

Kitchen stove and sink are separated by a safety buffer of 50cm

Technique #2 –
Beams Above Kitchen Stove

In Feng Shui principles, a protruding beam is a suppressive structure that can cause undesirable effects for people or objects situated underneath it. The kitchen stove is an important residence symbol that should never be placed directly under a structural beam.

In the event of such occurrence, problems related to family finances may occur, legal issues may arise for the male head of the family, and female family members can get physiological and phycological problems.

The remedy to such layout is to move the kitchen stove to another location away from the beams. If moving is not a convenient choice, hang an auspicious Feng Shui flute with a red string at either end of the beams to negate the suppressive Chi energy emanating from the beam.

An unfavorable kitchen setup where structural beams are directly above the stove

Technique #3 –
Size of Kitchen Entrance

The size of the kitchen entrance should always be smaller than the main entrance because the main door is the supposed inlet of Chi energy that enters the premise from the external environment. Therefore, for Chi energy to flow easily into the home, the primary door size should possess the biggest dimension to the other door sizes throughout the entire residence.

When a kitchen entrance is significantly larger than the main entrance, it signifies a misbalance of Chi energy proportion in the house. Problems like loss of monetary wealth, bickering and quarrel amongst couples, and poor job performance could surface for homeowners.

Although the main door should be larger in dimension, the kitchen entrance shouldn't be too small! Smaller-sized doors would otherwise constrict Chi energy and are unable to flow efficiently into the Kitchen compound. The delicate size ratio has to be calculated according to the dimension of the kitchen space and the entire house premise.

The size of the kitchen entrance shall be smaller than the main door

Technique #4 - Layout of Kitchen

When analyzing the Feng Shui landscape of a house, consideration of the shape of the kitchen is essential. It is advisable to adopt a square or rectangular shape kitchen instead of an irregular odd-shaped design. Because for regular-shape kitchen space, Chi energy is able to flow smoothly and evenly, distributing Chi energy to every side and angle.

In contrast, an irregular-shape kitchen layout could have multiple dead spots within the kitchen compound that are impossible for Chi energy to flow through and reach. When Chi energy in an area is interrupted by blockage or obstruction, the overall balance of Chi energy is disturbed and in a state of imperfection.

This imbalanced Chi energy resulting from the unfavourable kitchen shape layout can result in homeowners suffering poor health conditions, loss of wealth, and hindrance to career advancement.

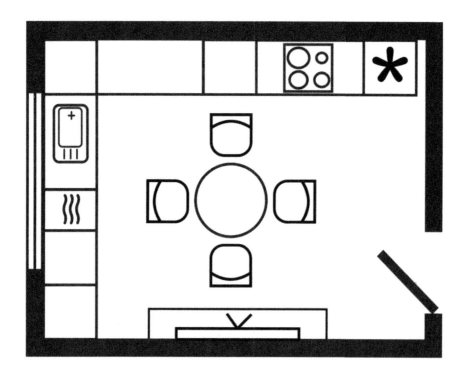

An ideal rectangular shape kitchen layout

Technique #5 -
Natural Light in Kitchen

In Feng Shui principles, light is associated with positive energy and represents the Fire element in the Five Elements Cycle. When the Fire element of a kitchen is adequately activated and boosted, positive vibe brewing from the kitchen compound can exuberate to different parts of the house.

Such activation is not possible when the kitchen space is dark and poorly lit. Therefore it is crucial to ensure adequate kitchen lighting surrounds the entire kitchen space to fill the house with positive energy and auspicious luck. It contributes to fostering an ideal atmosphere for homeowners to receive wealth and fortune with ease.

In addition, natural sunlight is preferred over lights source from electric-powered lamps. Therefore, homeowners should always open the window in the kitchen to allow natural sunshine to illuminate the kitchen compound at all times.

Kitchen area positively filled with natural sunlight

Technique #6 -
Sturdy Wall Behind Stove

For the stove's positioning, it is important to be backed by an entire solid and firm wall. From the Feng Shui perspective, having a strong backing for the kitchen stove symbolizes homeowners' ease at forming harmonious relationships in the job and gaining positive support from superiors. Brick should be the material for the whole wall instead of any flimsy material.

Homeowners should always note the rule of thumb for kitchen walls behind stove should be of substantial and sturdy material to receive good support and rapport at work. Therefore stove on a kitchen island or in front of windows is never a favored option from the philosophy studies of Feng Shui.

Kitchen stove backed by a firm and sturdy wall as support

Technique #7 - Location of Kitchen

In Fengshui principles, the Five Element Cycle plays a vital role in determining the suitable location for different parts of the residential area. The kitchen is represented by the Fire element, and as a general guide, it should ideally not be located in the North, Southwest, and Northeast segments of the residence.

Based on the Eight Trigrams Bagua, the North direction signifies the Water element, so a constant elemental clash between Fire and Water elements can happen when the kitchen resides in this location. An elemental clash is an inauspicious activity that is best avoided in the kitchen area.

The Southwest and Northeast directions signify the Earth element, and in the Five Element Cycle, the Earth element can weaken the Fire element of the kitchen. The important rule of thumb to take note of in kitchen space is it must be well boosted by Wood elements or Fire elements and not be 'destructed' by Water and Earth elements. A weakened Fire element of the kitchen compound will result in marital problems, loss of wealth for homeowners, and health problems for the female owner of the household.

The ideal locations for a kitchen area can be located in the East or Southeast position of the house as both directions belong to the Wood element and are considered favorable. Kitchen residing in these locations allows homeowners to enjoy greater financial luck and better health conditions.

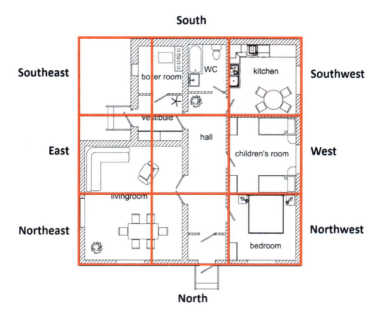

The kitchen is located in the inauspicious Southwest segment of the house

Technique #8 - Kitchen Stove And Door

Because the kitchen door is the portal where Chi energy flows towards the kitchen, the front area of the door has an influx of Chi energy circulating in high momentum. Therefore having the kitchen stove situated near or in front of the entrance should be avoided as it may cause a possible crash of Chi energy.

A folklore belief is that during the olden days in China, poverty was widespread amongst general commoners, so food was a symbol of prosperity and abundance in the family. Therefore the kitchen stove that prepares food is a signature representation of wealth and is generally hidden from the front sight of every guest that enters the house or kitchen compound.

As kitchen stove is an essential aspect of Feng Shui landform in every home residence, planning its position must be careful to avoid igniting any possible marital problems, health, and wealth issues with homestayers.

Kitchen stove is located too near to the kitchen door

Technique #9 -
Kitchen Equipment Placement

According to the classic Feng Shui manual, the kitchen stove is the main structure of the entire kitchen space that needs to be emphasized for its correct placement and usage. This concept may not hold water anymore in modern-day Feng Shui uses. Many alternate cooking devices like an electric rice cooker or microwave oven serve the same purpose of getting food cooked and prepared for the family meals. However, their exclusion from Feng Shui usage was because they weren't invented during ancient times.

Therefore in modern Feng Shui uses, homeowners should also consider the arrangement of this kitchenware as they can positively or adversely affect the luck of family members. Kitchen equipment such as microwave oven and rice cooker should be placed with the same Feng Shui guideline as a kitchen stove.

Rice cooker and microwave oven are as crucial as the stove in the kitchen compound

Technique #10 -
Toilet Above Kitchen Stove

In a multi-storied apartment home, it is vital to note that the kitchen stove should not be located under any toilet or bathroom on the upper level. Because the toilet or bathroom is primarily a Water element area, a Fire element kitchen stove situated beneath it may cause unwanted elemental clashes and damage to the prosperity energy surrounding it.

In addition, the toilet or bathroom compound accumulates and holds passive Yin energy, so it should not be located on top of the kitchen area that exuberates active Yang energy. They should be kept far apart, both in terms of horizontal and vertical distance as much as possible.

A negative Feng Shui configuration like this may cause homeowners to experience loss of wealth or problems related to heart or blood conditions to surface.

The toilet should never be directly located above the kitchen stove position.

Technique #11 - Kitchen Stove on Island

Many homeowners love to install stoves on a kitchen island these days, which are fashionable and functional. While it looks great, it may not be ideal for the kitchen stove because the kitchen island is a standalone structure in the middle of the kitchen space that signifies 'drifting or floating' without a stable support structure.

The position of the kitchen stove needs to be in a place that is 'rooted and stable,' so homeowners can accumulate wealth at ease and achieve stellar results in career progression. The recommended kitchen stove placement is to be in a location that has a solid wall behind its back or preferably next to a brick wall.

A kitchen island is not a good location to house a stove

Technique #12 - Golden Triangle Formation of Kitchen

One of my commonly used Feng Shui techniques in many house consultations is adapting the Golden Triangle Formation for the kitchen area. It is the formation where the three most important kitchen objects are strategically placed in three separate corners in a triangular fashion. This formation enhances Chi energy in the kitchen to be more auspicious and favorable.

The first corner of the formation is the kitchen stove. Responsible for food preparation for the family, it is undisputedly the most vital part of the kitchen space. The second corner of the formation is the water faucet. Water is a wealth attractor in Feng Shui study and an essential source of life. Last in the Golden Triangle Formation is the refrigerator. A place to store fresh food produce, it is regarded as the Storage of Wealth (财库) in the kitchen compound.

To achieve the best possible effect of the Golden Triangle Formation, the homeowner shall place the stove at the left corner of the triangle and the water faucet at the right corner. The refrigerator is placed in the upper-middle position, serving as a divider between the stove and the water faucet.

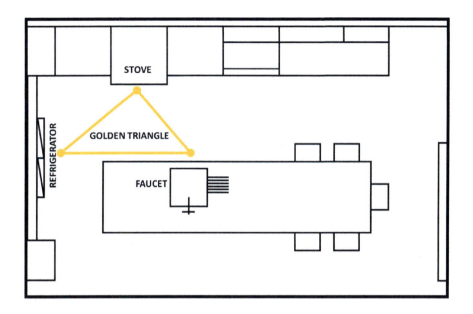

The auspicious Golden Triangle Formation in kitchen

Technique #13 -
Kitchen Behind Deity Altar

The living room space is usually the largest area in the entire house, with a wide, spacious, and bright area. Generally, it is the preferred spot for Buddhist or Taoist devotees to set up their deity altar, overlooking the external environment. During the consultation audit, many houses I came across have the kitchen space layout located right beside the living room area, sharing the same wall. This layout usually coincides with the position of the deity altar resting on this shared wall of the living room portion.

It is not an ideal Feng Shui configuration when the deity altar is positioned with its back facing the kitchen. Because kitchen compound exuberating strong active Yang Chi energy can constantly cause a stir and great disturbance to the surrounding energy vibe of the deity altar. According to Chinese customary beliefs and traditional Feng Shui studies, the deity altar space's location should be free of distractions, movement, and noise. The environment should be kept as silent as possible.

Inauspicious for the deity altar positioned with its back facing the kitchen area

Technique #14 - Open Concept Kitchen

Many homeowners in recent years have opted for an open kitchen space in a new-age house design where the kitchen seamlessly merges with the living room space without any borders, doors, or entrance attached. This layout is also prevalent in smaller-sized apartments with space constraint problem design.

From Feng Shui perspective, this is not a recommended layout. Because Chi energy moving around kitchen space needs to be rounded up and collected. With an open concept kitchen, Chi energy is free-roaming and is unable to power up kitchen space with the necessary active Yang Chi energy.

In addition, the kitchen entrance is an essential symbolic structure that can affect its homestayers' luck and personal life. Homeowners' wealth, luck, and career progression can be seriously hindered and affected without a proper kitchen entrance in an open concept design.

A typical open-concept kitchen without wall and door

Technique #15 - Kitchen and Bedroom Door

In most houses' design layouts, kitchen space is situated further away from the bedroom to avoid smoky fumes and greasy oil. However, due to some land constraint houses, both locations may be located near each other.

The natural characteristic of the kitchen compound is filled with dynamic and vibrant Chi energy, which stems from its active Yang activities such as cooking, washing, and cleaning. Therefore, kitchen space brimming with intense active Yang energy can create a nasty disturbance to the slow energy vibe within the bedroom. It is important to note that the kitchen door should never directly face the bedroom entrance in such a house layout.

When faced with this problem, check whether a gap distance of at least 2 meters is between the kitchen and bedroom doors. The adverse effects are negligible if they are more than 2 meters apart. However, suppose they are within this distance. One quick remedy is to ensure the bedroom door is always kept closed if you don't wish to make significant changes to the interior premise arrangement.

Kitchen compound located too close to the bedroom door

Technique #16 -
Hidden Kitchen From Main Door

In ancient China, poverty was widespread, and food was often scarce amongst the general public. Families with a constant food supply are often the target of burglars and thieves to their unguarded houses.

Therefore, it is common for the kitchen to be located in the back segment of the residence premise hidden from the public eyes. And in doing so, wealth and other assets can be well protected and preserved, allowing the family to prosper and thrive.

From Feng Shui philosophy, the kitchen shouldn't be situated near the front part of the house or visible from the main door entrance. It should ideally be located at the back of the house, preferably behind a privacy wall that protects it from the sight of the front door.

Kitchen area located at the back of the house and not visible from the main entrance

Technique #17 -
Keeping Kitchen Clean and Tidy

One golden rule in maintaining good Feng Shui across the entire house is ensuring the kitchen area remains clean and tidy. Food remnants are a common sight in the food preparation and cooking process. If they are not appropriately removed, bacteria will proliferate, insects and rodents may manifest in these areas.

Unclean and unhygienic kitchen space breeds terrible smell and sight, creating negative Chi energy around the house. Even if the external and internal Feng Shui landform is optimal at attracting auspicious Chi energy, a dirty and foul-smelling area can override these existing features and turn positive Chi energy into unwanted negative energy.

Simply said, unclean kitchen space can result in bad Feng Shui energy vibe that is worse than the bathroom!

A clean and tidy kitchen space is essential for maintaining its good Feng Shui

Technique #18 -
Direct Sunlight on Kitchen Stove

Natural sunlight is highly preferred in the kitchen compound as it illuminates the entire area with positive active Yang energy. However, when sunlight rays shine directly on the kitchen stove surface, it becomes more bane than a boon.

Because sunlight contains harmful UV rays that degrade and discolor materials over time, the kitchen stove can get damaged from this prolonged exposure. Remember, the kitchen stove is an imperative structure of the kitchen space and must remain in its best condition at all times.

In addition, if the sunlight is from the West-Sun direction or more commonly known as the Afternoon Sun, they are considered Water element sunlight that can create potent problems for homeowners. Health, wealth, and relationships can be adversely affected by this negative Feng Shui arrangement in the kitchen.

Avoid locating the kitchen stove at places where direct sunlight may permeate through

Technique #19 -
Position Level of Kitchen Stove

The kitchen stove should always be on the same level with the countertop platform height throughout the kitchen.

When kitchen stoves are built lower or on a low-set platform, this can result in the loss of wealth, investment opportunities, and financial hardship for homeowners. On the other hand, when kitchen stoves are built higher than the countertop platform, family members feel suppressed and limit their growth potential in work or academic fields.

From Feng Shui philosophy, the kitchen stove needs to be maintained at the correct height level. Many are not aware that the height level of the kitchen stove and countertop can affect the state of energy vibe in the kitchen space. When the energy vibe is adversely affected, family members can experience health and wealth-related problems.

Kitchen stove on a low-set platform is not auspicious

Technique #20 - Kitchen Stove Sandwiched Between Water Objects

In the context of the Five Element Cycle studies, the Water element 'destructs' the Fire element the same way as how water can extinguish fire sources in real life. A water faucet, refrigerator, and washing machine are known as Water element appliances. It is essential to note that the kitchen stove, which belongs to the Fire element, should not be sandwiched between these Water element equipment.

When two Water element appliances are situated on both sides of the kitchen stove, their Water elemental presence can damage the Fire element quality of the stove. Any elemental damage signifies an adverse state to the energy vibe of the entire kitchen space.

Such placement creates an unfavorable Feng Shui setting as the fire stove is the vital component representing the heart and soul of the kitchen compound. Therefore keeping them apart will prevent unwanted celestial clashes between these two elements in the kitchen space and improve the entire Chi energy of the kitchen.

Do not be confused between this sandwiched position and the Golden Triangle Formation, which requires the stove, faucet, and refrigerator to form up in a triangular position. If the kitchen stove is found to be in this sandwiched position, a buffer zone of at least 50cm on each side can smoothen the effect of such undesirable elemental clashes.

Fire stove sandwiched between Water element appliances with sufficient buffer space

Chapter 3:
Feng Shui Techniques for Living Room

The living room space has always been a fundamental component of any home. Whether living alone or with family, it is the common area where most social gatherings and family events take place in a house.

It is often necessary to have a living space brimming with positive Chi energy for the general well-being of occupiers. By adhering to the principles of good Feng Shui philosophy in the living room premises, homeowners can achieve a tremendous difference in their quality of life. The living room may not be the first segment of the house one thinks about enhancing with Feng Shui, but it plays an important role that shouldn't be ignored.

The living room is where everyone gathers, whether its family and friends or associates from various groups. It is also a location where both guest and host can enjoy a drink, engage in conversation, relax over TV programs, or read books. Thus, the key to keeping this place in good Feng Shui is to make sure it exudes positive and vibrant Chi energy that is both welcoming and comfortable to everyone who steps in.

Technique #21 - Living Room at Front of House

The layout arrangement of the house is of critical importance in the application of good Feng Shui. The living room space should be ideally located at the front of the main door, followed by other segments of the house like the kitchen, bedroom, and toilet space.

When Chi energy enters through the main house door from the external environment, the living room holds an important task of collecting and retaining it with its large spaces. Therefore, positioning the living room area at the front of the house is essential to effectively gather Chi energy straight from the entrance and redistribute it to the other house segment.

If the living room is not optimally situated at the front of the residence, Chi energy doesn't get effectively retained when it enters. This can result in an outflow of Chi energy that is bad for the Feng Shui design creating an unsuitable place for living.

Living room ideally situated near the front entrance and well connected to rest of the house

Technique #22 - Sofa Positioning

The sofa is undoubtedly the centerpiece furniture for most residential homes. It is also the most utilized furniture in the living room where most family members and guests occupy long hours for TV, chit-chatting, or socializing purposes.

A sofa positioned with a solid and sturdy wall behind is in tandem with Feng Shui philosophy of having strong support for seating furniture to harbor a harmonious relationship among family members.

It is also highly preferable if a corner space is available in the living room for the sofa to reside in, as it is an excellent layout to be tucked in such a corner surrounded by wall support. From Feng Shui's perspective, Chi energy flowing in the living room can be easily retained and collected in such configuration leading to a prosperous energy vibe within the area.

However, not every living room space is feasible for sofas to be back-facing walls or sit inside corners. In that case, any big and sturdy furniture placed behind it can effectively simulate the strong support for sofa furniture.

Sofa placement is highly preferred when residing in the corner of the living room

Technique #23 - Avoid Low Ceiling

It is ideal to avoid a living room with a low ceiling because it creates an oppressive feeling for those gathering around the area. When people around feel constricted in the space, negative vibes start brewing, affecting the energy vibe around the compound.

To ensure the ceiling has optimal space for living, it is best to avoid having any furniture with overhanging decorations or installing a fake ceiling wall that can visually reduce the ceiling height. However, these are not an issue if you live in a big residence equipped with a high ceiling to accommodate these modifications.

When the ceiling is low and the living room is small, it is hard to harness the excellent Feng Shui energy around the residence. Therefore, as a general rule of thumb, keep the living room airy and spacious by avoiding a low ceiling in the compound.

Avoid low ceiling area for living room compound

Technique #24 -
Carpet for Feng Shui Improvement

Carpets are undoubtedly one of the most accessible accessories for changing the Feng Shui of a residence. They often cover a large area and occupy the dominant center position in the living room. The color and pattern of the carpet, if well matched, can enhance the quality of Chi energy required by the household.

Homeowners can use the color patterns of the carpet to bring luck to the residence. Patterns have their own individual characteristics and meanings according to the Five Element Cycle: wave shape is Water element, straight stripes are Wood element, stars and colorful patterns are Fire element, lattice patterns are Earth element and circles shapes are Metal element. The carpets can be well oriented and colored to bring good fortune to the entire family.

Carpet with circular pattern designs for inducing Metal element to the living room space

Technique #25 -
Carpet with Auspicious Colour and Pattern

Most apartments' main doors directly open up to the living room segment of a residence. Placing a suitable carpet at the main entrance that matches the door's location in the house can positively enhance the overall luck of homeowners.

- Main Door at South of Residence - Placing red carpet with straight stripes or star-shaped patterns in this direction enhances the family with positive energy and good fortune.
- Main Door at East or Southeast of Residence – Placing green carpet with a wave or straight pattern can help homeowners improve interpersonal relationships.
- Main Door at Southwest or Northeast of Residence – Placing a yellow carpet with a star-like pattern in this direction can bring prosperous wealth and enhance marital bliss.
- Main Door at North of Residence - Placing rectangular or wavy blue carpet in this direction can help to improve career luck by assisting homeowners in finding a good job and increasing their chance of promotion at work.
- Main Door at West or Northwest of Residence – Placing white or gold carpet with a checkered pattern in this direction can bring forth prosperous wealth luck to the homeowners and enhance children's learning capability.

Recommended to have rectangular blue carpet when the main door is at North of the residence

Technique #26 - Identifying Wealth Position

One of the most important segments of a residential premise is undoubtedly the Wealth Position of a house. This area can generate wealth, luck and grant prosperity and abundance to homeowners when it is correctly located.

There are numerous ways to identify the wealth position of a residence premise, such as using Xuan Kong Flying Stars and Eight Mansions which are advanced methodologies that require a deeper understanding of the Feng Shui fundamentals. For ease of understanding, we will be using the more straightforward and effective Front Door Wealth Corner method in this book to identify the house's primary wealth spots.

To locate the wealth sector, one has to stand from the front door location and look diagonally across the living room in a 45 degrees direction. The wealth area will be situated at the opposite end of the diagonal line of sight. For an important note, the diagonal line of sight stretching from the main door to the wealth spot must be unblocked and clearly visible when standing from the front door.

Which direction should the diagonal line pan? The direction of the diagonal line can pan either left or right, depending on which way the main door swings;

- The front door opens to the left – The diagonal line pans 45 degrees to the right, and the wealth position is located at the opposite end of the diagonal line.
- The front door opens to the right – The diagonal line pans 45 degrees to the left, and the wealth position is located at the opposite end of the diagonal line.

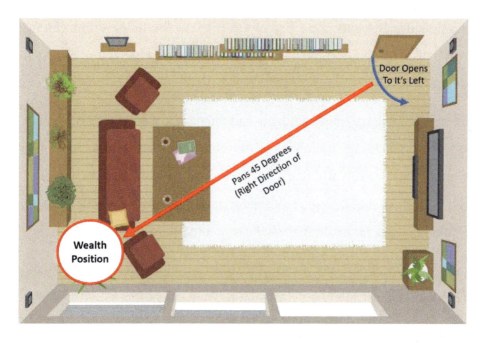

Wealth Position is located at the opposite end of the 45 degrees diagonal line from the main door

Technique #27 -
Keeping Windows Open

Most residential living rooms have several windows panels for air circulation purposes, but some homeowners choose to open them occasionally. Reasons were usually to prevent the house from getting dusty, or air conditioning usage has replaced the need for an open window.

I always emphasize to my students and clients the importance of getting windows open despite their reasons or living habits. Because a constantly opened window critically helps in the circulation process of Chi energy within the household. In the study Feng Shui philosphy, having good air circulation in a house is essential for maintaining an excellent living environment.

When Chi energy enters a premise, it must get out efficiently for a new wave of Chi energy to re-enter and complete the circulation procedure. The exit outlets of Chi energy are usually these opened windows that help remove negative Chi energy and induce positive Chi energy into the household.

This circulation process ensures the premise is not surrounded by stale and stagnant Chi energy, which can cause health and wealth woes to homeowners.

Living room with open window ideal for circulation of Chi energy

Technique #28 - A Bright Living Room

A good dose of active Yang energy helps occupants feel positive and energized with vitality, and often a bright living room is a crucial key that attracts such energy to this space. For homeowners to unwind and socialize comfortably at home, the living area should be brimming with positive Chi energy from the environment's illuminating sunlight.

In a recent study, researchers discovered the brightness of an area has a significant impact on the psychological aspect of its user. When a living room is dimly lighted, occupiers are more prone to conflict, arguments, and disputes within the family. A dimly lighted living space also encourages the development of a ruminating mind. Rumination is associated with mental and physical health problems, such as depression and anxiety, which can lead to long-term mental health issues.

The use of natural sunlight is the most preferred method for brightening up the entire living room space. If it is not possible to have sufficient natural lighting in the living room, use alternatives like the placement of skylights or artificial light that brightens the room with no flicker or glare.

Bright living room with natural sunlight is ideal for attracting positive Chi energy to the area

Technique #29 - Walkway Behind Sofa

From Feng Shui's perspective, homeowners should ideally place the sofa back-facing a sturdy wall or a huge piece of furniture like a cabinet wall that resembles firm and robust support. However, if it's not feasible for one, it is essential to note that the sofa should never be placed in a direction back-facing a walkway or an alley in the living room.

This is primarily because such a passageway has constant moving energy (caused by the movement generated in the walkway) that is unfit for an area behind the sofa. This area is more preferred for slow-moving Chi energy vibes by the placement of prominent fixtures or furniture.

A passageway behind sofa arrangements can result in homeowners suffering from a disharmonious relationship in their working environment and a lack of access to support and resources when pursuing their goals in life.

The back of the sofa should not face the passageway in the living room

Technique #30 -
Fireplace in Living Room

According to the classic Feng Shui philosophy, frequent use of the fireplace located in the Northwest sector of the living room can adversely affect the health conditions of male family members of the household. According to the Five Element Cycle studies, a strong Fire elemental presence exuding from the fireplace can readily 'destruct' the Metal element presence, representing male individuals in the family.

Men over the age of 45 or who have health concerns such as abnormalities with the heart and blood vessels, including excessive blood pressure, cardiovascular illness, are to be extra careful with their health if this formation is present in their residence.

In addition, if the fireplace is located in the West sector of the living room, frequent usage of the fireplace can result in money problems such as difficulty in accumulating wealth and income generation for homeowners. If this formation exits in the living room, minimize the use of the fireplace or set up an electric heater in other locations to cut down the effects of the problems.

Fireplace shall be placed at auspicious sector of the living room to avoid health and wealth problems

Technique #31 - Sofa Under Beams

Beams are a structural feature in both the interior and exterior of buildings. Their uses are indispensable as they serve to support the structural frame of the building, similar to the functions of pillars. However, in Feng Shui's perspective, beams are a much-shunned feature in a residential home.

Consistent with Feng Shui practices regarding overhead beams in kitchen and bedroom design, homeowners should avoid structural beams for all important areas in residence, including sofa couches in the living room.

When a structural beam is directly above the sofa area, it creates an air of uneasiness caused by the negative Chi energy generated by the suppressive beams. Prolonged exposure to this Chi energy can cause undesirable emotional and psychological effects for people seated beneath it. In the long run, the presence of any overhead beams over one's living room sofa can bring about the negative influences of misfortune, sickness, and bad luck to the homeowners.

Sofa is not recommended to be placed under structural beams in the living room

Technique #32 - Ceiling and Flooring Relationship

In the residential living room area, the ceiling and flooring have a symbiotic relationship representing the passive Yin (阴) and active Yang (阳)of the Eight Trigrams Bagua(八卦), or Heaven and Earth, respectively. Because of this relationship, their colors and design should match according to the principles of Eight Trigrams Bagua, which emphasizes maintaining the delicate balance of energy in the Yin and Yang realm.

As the ceiling is symbolic of Heavenly cosmic energy while the flooring represents Earthly energy, the overall color of the ceiling should appear and feel lighter than the color of the flooring tiles. Colors such as white or turquoise can be used on the top, while homeowners can choose heavier colors like brown or grey for flooring.

From Feng Shui's design perspective, the ceiling can be painted a light shade with some intricate patterns or crisp or clean-cut designs, creating a feeling of exuberance and openness. On the contrary, flooring tiles can have heavier and deeper colors bringing calmness and strength to the living room space.

If it is hard to adopt such a color scheme design, a more straightforward method is simply having the flooring tiles color shade darker than the ceiling top. So long as a difference of color shade is present, it will suffice.

Simple colour scheme difference with white ceiling and light brown flooring is most ideal

Technique #33 -
Cluttering Accumulates Negative Chi

Cluttering is often the culprit for the gradual build-up of negative Chi energy in the residential premise. When obstruction of land space caused by cluttering takes up a significant presence, it disrupts the smooth circulation of positive Chi energy around the house. Uncirculated Chi energy then turns into a negative form over time.

Cluttering has the worst effect when it is present in the living room compound. As this area is usually well connected and easily accessible to other segments of the residence, it can quickly spread negative Chi energy around the house like a transmittable virus.

The remedy solution to such a problem is to practice decluttering. It is recognized as a simple but effective means of eliminating negative and unfavorable energy vibes from the living quarters.

The first step of decluttering is primarily getting rid of unnecessary objects or categorizing stuff that is not usable anymore. Chuck them away or recycle them into valuable materials. The next step is keeping useful items in big and well-labeled storage boxes for easier access in the future. Keep them neatly in a storage room and out of sight.

It is essential to declutter the house at least twice a month to ensure the living space is clutter-free and flowing with positive Chi energy.

Auspicious luck can be quickly introduced into homeowners' life when the place is brimming with a good energy vibe.

Avoid cluttered living room space that breeds negative Chi energy

Technique #34 - Pillar in Living Room

Pillars are not a recommended structure found in a residential living room as they can create negative interior Feng Shui landforms. They are seen as an obstacle to homeowners as their presence can drastically obstruct the ideal flow of Chi energy throughout the living room space. According to classical Feng Shui, a pillar structure is akin to a dagger piercing right through the heart in the middle of the residential premise.

Ideally, living room space should be free of any structures or huge building blocks. When homeowners live in a property with such features, they may feel financially pressured and likely have medical diseases related to the stomach region.

Such configuration in a house is not suitable for children and teenagers as it can cause them to lack motivation and confidence in school, making them less likely to do well academically. Another major drawback of having pillar in the living room is that it might create tensions in relationships between family members.

Avoid having pillar in the middle of the living room space

Technique #35 - Placement of Huge Live Plants

Although having plants in the home is beneficial to relieve tension and fatigue, the placement of big live plants in the living room may not be ideal in some instances where Feng Shui orientation is concerned.

Homeowners should not place huge live plants in the Southwest or Northeast sector of the house if the living room is in these locations. Because the Southwest and Northeast directions are associated with Earth elements, and plants that are representative of Wood elements 'destruct' Earth elements.

According to the fundamental principles of the Five Elements Cycle, a destructive relationship between two elements is not favored and should be avoided at best. Homeowners should follow guidelines adhering to this metaphysical concept to harness its positive effect and prevent the negative from manifesting.

The digestive system of household members can be affected if a huge plant is situated near the Northeast corner of a Northeast-facing living room. Female family members may also suffer psychological and physical health issues if large plants are placed in the Southwest corner of a living room.

If it is necessary to place some plants in these areas, make sure that small plants don't take up much space. Additionally, fake plants are more preferred to live plants when considering placement in these unfavorable spots.

Avoid having huge live plants in living room if its situated in Southwest or Northeast sector of the house

Furnitures Arrangement

There are two golden rules in the Feng Shui aspect that need to be adhered to when considering furniture arrangement. First is the choice of suitable furniture size and second, is making adequate spaces between furniture.

Furniture takes up a majority of space in the living room compound, and their arrangement can affect the nature of Chi energy movement. Understanding and applying these fundamental golden rules in the living room are essential for all homeowners interested in enhancing their luck.

Technique #36 and Technique #37 are applicable under Furniture Arrangement topic.

Technique #36 - Suitable Furniture Size

The furniture size and dimension have to be in the correct ratio with the size of the living room. If the living room space is small and constrained, the choice of furniture has to be relatively modest with the allocated space. In retrospect, a huge bungalow with an enormous living room compound can have the luxury of bigger size furniture to fit in.

Who gets big and oversized furniture when they have a small living space? The fact is that there are cases where ill-fitting furniture is purchased, not knowing that they constitute a bad Feng Shui design for the entire house.

For example, one homeowner placed a seven-seater sofa set in a small apartment that takes up most of the space in the living room. The purchase was because the leather sofa was on a substantial seasonal discount, so it was bought at a snap, not considering the design suitability.

Avoid having large furniture in a small living room space

Technique #37 - Making Spaces

During furniture arrangement, always ensure sufficient space and gaps are present between each of them for effective circulation of Chi energy in the living room. When multiple pieces of furniture were placed together with no gaps, it resembled a stumbling block in the living room space that impedes and restricts the movement of Chi energy. A gap distance of at least 30 to 50 cm is required when considering the placement of furniture.

However, not all furniture arrangement is applicable to this guideline. Custom-built furniture that is fitted to the wall's recess area does not require any gap distance. For example, a stretch of cabinets, feature wall, and tv console stand built into the recessed area of the living room that flushes with the surrounding wall does not pose a problem from Feng Shui's perspective. Chi energy doesn't get affected in this type of design arrangement.

Custom built furniture that sits in recess area of living room increases circulation of Chi energy

Auspicious Painting in Living Room

Having art pieces displayed in the living room increases the aesthetic senses of the area. Painting, which is appealing to the eyes and often colorful, has the capacity to change the ambiance of an area. From Feng Shui's perspective, hanging the right type of art painting can give specific benefits for homeowners. Here are several pointers for enhancing the living room with good Feng Shui painting.

Technique #38, Technique #39 and Technique #40 are applicable under Auspicious Painting in Living Room topic.

Technique #38 -
Avoid Painting with Weapons or Firearms

Weapons such as knives, guns, or axes should be avoided in painting. As they are dangerous firearms in nature, they can bring an undesirable negative energy vibe to the living room. Words, quotes, portraits, or symbols that represent negative emotions such as sadness or anger should be avoided by and large as well.

Avoid having painting of a revolver in the middle of the living room

Technique #39 -
Auspicious Painting with Nine Koi Fishes

It is auspicious for a painting to encompass nine koi fishes in the water in the Feng Shui world. Fish has always been frequently utilized as a good luck symbol, as its Chinese pronunciation "Yu" can be translated as Surplus and Abundance in its meanings. In addition, fish are said to be water-bound, and in Feng Shui's perspective, water denotes prosperity and wealth. Therefore, a painting with Nine Koi Fishes in the living room symbolizes longevity, an abundance of wealth, and smooth sailing for all future endeavors to the homestayers of the premise.

Painting of Nine Koi Fishes in the middle of the living room is highly recommended

Technique #40 - Auspicious Painting with Dragon and Phoenix

The dragon symbolizes the principle of active Yang for males and represents the idea of masculinity; the phoenix symbolizes the principle of passive Yin for females and illustrates the idea of femininity. The dragon and phoenix symbolize the peace and joy that are associated with a happy marital life. Good luck and auspiciousness is conveyed by the dragon and phoenix motif as well.

Therefore, a painting with Dragon and Phoenix in living room can help married couple achieve marital harmony as well as abundance of auspicious luck for the family.

Painting of Dragon and Phoenix in the middle of the living room increase marital harmony

Chapter 4: Feng Shui Techniques for Bedroom

In Feng Shui's perspective, the bedroom is viewed as one of the most significant rooms in the home. It's the place you are likely to spend the most time in for sleeping and resting, so it is essential to maximize the Feng Shui benefit in this room as much as possible.

As it's a place meant for relaxing and rejuvenation, a bedroom with positive Chi energy flow can have a tremendous healing effect on the body and mind. The primary focus in bedroom Feng Shui lies in getting the right type of Chi to flow within and making sure the arrangement and direction of bed location are proper according to Feng Shui philosophy.

Amongst the entire living space, the bedroom is usually the most private and personal space for individuals and married couples. Therefore, ensuring the Feng Shui arrangement in the bedroom is optimal can significantly enhance marital bliss and increase relationship luck for occupants.

Door Facing Bed

Obtaining an auspicious position for the bed is considered the number one priority for the bedroom premises. Just like a sofa's position in the living room and the stove's positioning in the kitchen, the center of focus in achieving a good Feng Shui arrangement for the bedroom ought to be the placement of the bed.

The bedroom door is considered the portal of Chi energy flowing inwards of the bedroom, so its position to the bed has immense significance when analyzing the room's layout. The following are several pointers between the door and bed facing for ensuring prominent Chi energy is flowing consistently in the bedroom.

Technique #41 and Technique #42 are applicable under Door Facing Bed topic.

Technique #41 - Bedroom Door Facing Bed

The bedroom door entrance should not be directly facing the foot and head of the bed. According to the Feng Shui philosophy, this type of bed arrangement will lead to health concerns for homeowners. Headaches, migraines, and other symptoms related to the upper body will arise when the bedroom door is oriented toward the top of the bed. Additionally, knee difficulties or a sprain are likely to occur when one is lying on a bed with their feet facing the entrance position.

Avoid having bedroom door directly facing the foot of the bed

Technique #42 -
Toilet Door Facing Bed

The toilet door residing in the bedroom should never be directly facing the foot and head of the bed. Similar to the adverse effect when the bedroom door is facing the bed, this configuration is much deadlier as the toilet compound is a breeding space for negative Chi energy that can create serious health issues for homeowners. Problems related to mental health, kidneys, lungs, and lower parts of the body are likely to occur for occupiers in such a bedroom configuration.

Avoid having toilet door directly facing the foot of the bed

Technique #43 - Avoid Poison Arrow Chi

In Feng Shui philosophy, Poison Arrow Chi is being characterized as a forceful and negative Sha Chi 煞气 (Killing Energy) that typically originates from pointed objects or structures with sharp edges. Homeowners should always avoid them in the entire residential premises, especially in the bedroom area. As it's a place for resting and rejuvenating, occupiers are more vulnerable to this negative energy during their sleeping period and should be extra cautious of these deadly formations.

Poison Arrow Chi is more dangerous than other unfavorable Feng Shui configurations because it can cause serious health problems to the occupiers of the bedroom. If the bedroom is constantly under these negative and forceful energies, chronic disease or terminal illness may develop over time.

Poison Arrow Chi can come from sharp edges of cabinets, overhead beams structure, or sharp protruding corners of the room. Always ensure that these negative Sha Chi are not directly pointed in the direction of the bed. If it does, one quick remedy is to cover them up with plants or smoothen the sharp edges with a tool.

Avoid having Poison Arrow Chi pointing towards the bed

Technique #44 - Declutter The Bedroom

The most common cause of a negative Chi energy flow in the bedroom is often linked to a cluttered and messy space created by unnecessary furniture, storage, and displaced items around the room. Cluttering is messy groups of things on the floor that impede the regular flow of Chi energy in an area like a blockage. This result in positive Chi energy eventually gets turned into negative Chi energy from the stagnation and immobility created by cluttering.

The analogy is similar to having a choked drainage system that is unable to dispel water out of its pipe. Over time, the water trapped within turns foul due to the inbreeding of bacteria and germs in its stagnant water. This still water represents the negative energy generated by the Chi energy flow blocked in a bedroom compound.

As the bedroom represents relationship and health, a cluttered, messy, and disorganized bedroom can create disharmonious relationships amongst family members and breed health problems for the occupants. Therefore, always make it a habit to declutter the home as frequently as possible or simply keep non-essential and frivolous items from entering the bedroom in the first place. Alternatively, have some built-in closets and storage drawers for effective and efficient storage.

Avoid having a cluttered and messy bedroom that blocks the regular flow of Chi energy

Technique #45 -
Space Under Bed

One often overlooked spot is the unused space underneath the bed that can affect the bedroom's Feng Shui conditions. Most beds are equipped with four supporting stands at each corner, creating ample area beneath them. Many homeowners like storing their belongings in this unblocked space to maximize usage in the bedroom. This practice is prevalent in countries where scarce land space and houses are tiny and expensive.

As much as this unuse space is ideal for storing items, the recommended Feng Shui configuration is to free up this area and have no stuff under the bed. The empty spaces allow Chi energy to flow freely in the bedroom space without any blockage. When positive Chi energy can roam around with no hindrance, stagnant and negative Chi energy doesn't build up in the bedroom space. This is essential for the healing and rejuvenation of the occupier's mind and body during the sleep process where positive Chi energy is present.

If it is necessary to utilize this underneath space for storage purposes, consider the kinds of stuff to be stored and scrutinize the objects in detail. When occupiers are asleep in bed, they are in a passive Yin energy state. Electronics or unclean things underneath the mattresses can adversely affect the quality of sleep. It is advisable to store items related to bedroom usage such as blankets, pillows, mattress covers to ensure an undisturbed rest throughout the night.

Ideal to free up spaces under bed without storage of items

Technique #46 -
Avoid Large Exposed Mirrors

Mirrors are standard pieces of furniture found in the bedroom. However, when placing large size or body-length mirrors, it is advisable to check the suitable areas for placement. In Feng Shui philosophy, mirrors can reflect and vibrate the surrounding energy due to their reflecting nature. And as the bedroom is a place of passive Yin energy space, such vibrancy caused by mirrors is to be avoided. When placing mirrors in unsuitable areas, problems related to infidelity in a relationship or breakdown of a marriage may occur.

As a rule of thumb, large mirrors should never be placed at the foot of a bed or facing a bed's headboard. Homeowners should also avoid areas close to the bed or within the reflecting range of the bed. If it is necessary to place large mirrors in the bedroom, be sure to hide them in a closet or cabinet that can be accessed with a swinging door. Alternatively, choose a smaller mirror that can be snug away in a corner when not in use.

Avoid having large mirror placed at the foot of a bed in bedroom

Technique #47 -
Bedroom Door Facing Door

In an apartment layout, having a bedroom door facing another bedroom door, toilet door, or other entrance is not an ideal configuration. Because when Chi energy flows into a bedroom, it is essential to remain in the area as long as possible. By allowing Chi energy to move and circulate around slowly, occupants can harness the positive benefits of a balanced Chi flow in the bedroom.

However, when another door entrance is situated just opposite the bedroom door, the Chi energy entering the bedroom gets pulled out before circulating the area. This can result in an erratic flow of Chi energy that is not favorable for a bedroom compound. Occupants may experience constant problems in marriage or relationships in such a bedroom configuration.

One quick remedy for such formation is to keep either one of the affected doors closed at all times. The preferred door to be closed should be the one that is more seldomly used, such as the toilet or storage room. In addition, if the distance between the two doors is wide and apart, the adverse effect is not particularly significant and can be considered negligible.

Two bedroom door directly facing each other is not an ideal configuration

Technique #48 -
Bedroom Door Facing Sharp Edges

The bedroom door is the portal where Chi energy enters and leaves the bedroom premises. When sharp edges of a wall or Poison Arrow Chi are found right outside of the bedroom door, it turns positive Chi energy entering the room into negative Sha Chi (Killing Energy).

From Feng Shui's perspective, this is a deadly configuration as occupants constantly absorb any negative Chi energy flowing within the room, resulting in deteriorating health problems and the possible development of chronic diseases. In addition, homeowners get 'sliced up' at the entrance by the sharp protruding edges whenever entering or leaving the room, which can cause constant bickering among couples, infidelity problems in marriage, and communication breakdown in relationships.

Therefore, it is advisable to remove the sharp edges outside of the room to avoid problems caused by the Poison Arrow Chi. One way is to engage a renovation contractor to smoothen the sharp edges of the wall or place potted plants directly in front of the sharp edges to block out any negative Sha Chi energy.

However, note that if the distance between the door and the edges of the wall is near, it is not recommended to have potted plants as they can cause blockage of Chi energy at the entrance. In such a situation, use a stretch of vine leaf to cover up the entire length of sharp edges, which can effectively prevent negative Sha Chi energy from affecting the room's occupants.

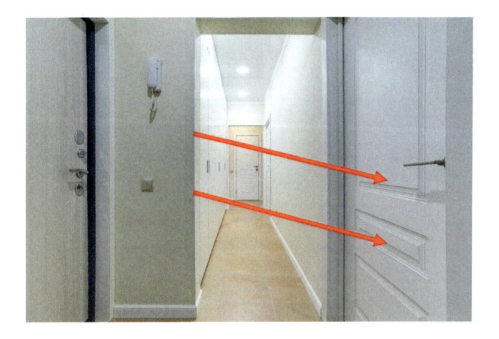

Avoid having sharp edges pointing towards bedroom door from outside

Technique #49 - Bed Under Low Ceiling

The bed should not be situated under a low ceiling as it can create a suffocating and pressurized effect on the occupants. The Feng Shui philosophy is similar to the unfavorable placement of beds under beam structures that can exert an intense, forceful, undesirable energy on the occupiers in the bedroom compound.

Low ceiling refers to ceilings with low height, resulting in them being too close to one's head or the bed. It is often caused by the attachment of a fake ceiling compartment to the ceiling façade that decreases the distance between ground and ceiling. The major concern of having low ceilings in the bedroom space is the circulation of negative Chi energy rampant in such bedroom layouts that can lead to serious health problems for the occupiers.

Therefore when choosing the preferred bedroom compound of the house, it is best to avoid occupying a room of such configuration. If absolutely necessary, make sure the bed's mattress is at least 3 meters away from the ceiling. Homeowners can achieve this by lowering the height of the bed frame by making some adjustments to the bed stand. This simple alternation can sufficiently protect homeowners from the adverse influence and effects of negative Chi forces.

Avoid having low ceiling above bed that can cause suffocating and pressurized effect on the occupants

Technique #50 - Shape of Room

From Feng Shui philosophy, it is always important to have a square or rectangle bedroom as far as possible. Rooms with these shapes often have a better balanced of Chi energy flowing within that is suitable for sleeping activities in the bedroom.

Homeowners should avoid oval, triangular, or odd shape rooms for bedroom layout as these shapes have imbalanced Chi energy flow, which is unsuitable for sleeping or resting. Rooms with these shapes often result in erratic Chi energy flow that is not ideal for occupants. Square and rectangular shapes are the preferred choices as they also represent Earth elements in the study of the Five Elements Cycle, which can be translated as stability and stillness energy vibe suitable for the bedroom activity.

Selecting a bedroom space with a square or rectangular layout can help shield some potential negative energy that may seriously impact the occupant's health. Another reason for avoiding rooms with odd shape designs is the possible presence of Poison Arrow Chi from the edges of the wall or corner. When such negative Sha Chi and imbalance of Chi energy flow is present in the same room, that can create significant problems for occupants.

Ideal to have a square shape bedroom with balanced Chi energy flow

Technique #51 - Avoid Water Feature

One common technique used to enhance Feng Shui home interior suggests installing water feature to improve various sectors of the house premise to achieve luck improvement effect. This concept is generally effective for some part of the house, but its usage adaptation in the bedroom compound is not recommended from a Feng Shui's perspective.

This is because the nature of Chi energy in the bedroom is slow and calm moving, as it's a place of passive Yin energy vibe. However, a water feature with a running water constantly stimulates and turns the surrounding Chi energy into an active and vibrant energy vibe. This mismatch of Chi energy orientation results in a space unsuitable for homeowners to reside in for long hours of resting and sleeping. If they continue to stay in the room for a prolonged period, occupants can experience problems with their minds, health, and bodies.

In addition, sound generated by the water features in the bedroom, such as a faucet dripping noise and water flowing sound, can cause continuous sound vibrations that are a form of negative Chi energy. Being exposed to this negative energy for an extended time can lead to psychological issues and mental health problems.

Large water feature unsuitable for bedroom area

Technique #52 - Getting a Headboard for Bed

Having a headboard for the bed may not be a preferred choice for every homeowner. However, considering the positive effects it can bring to the occupiers, it is clearly an essential item to be equipped with.

A headboard is situated above the head position of the bed, and having a good quality board can signify additional stability and support in a person's career and personal life. A recommended headboard is sturdy and made of rugged, solid material without any perforations. Always make sure the headboard is securely fastened to the bed, so it is not shaking or loosely secured.

A headboard is best backed by a solid brick wall instead of an empty space or other furniture from the Feng Shui philosophy. An empty or void space between the headboard and the wall allows negative Chi energy to gather around the bedroom, making occupiers feel restless and uneasy. Once this happens, the bedroom Feng Shui can be negatively affected. It is recommended to close up the gap space and ensure positive Chi energy is able to flow freely within the bedroom space.

One important note is ensuring that the other end of the solid wall is not occupied by any toilet or kitchen compound. When this configuration is present, it can cause mental stress, relationship problems, and sleep deprivation to the occupier of the bedroom.

Recommended to have bed with a thick and sturdy headboard back by a solid wall

Technique #53 - Avoid Bed Under Window

The window is known as the secondary portal within the bedroom for Chi energy to enter the house premise, while the door entrance is often regarded as the primary portal. Chi energy entering the bedroom space must be enhanced by the bed position to achieve a good energy flow in the area.

From Feng Shui philosophy, the head and foot of the bed should not face any window opening. If the bed faces a window in these configurations, it can expose the occupier to strong Chi energy present in the external part of the house. Sleeping is considered a passive Yin energy activity that needs to be coupled with slow Chi energy flow around the bed. And as these window openings are gateway portals for Chi energy movement, its vibrating and robust energy is unsuitable for the body and mind to rejuvenate from the sleep process.

The Chi energy moving in these areas must be tranquil to have a deep, sound, and refreshing sleep. Therefore, the bed position mustn't face any window opening to ensure a good Feng Shui layout in the bedroom space.

Not ideal for head of bed to back-face a window opening

Technique #54 -
Avoid Fixtures Above Bed

Just like structural beams or low ceilings directly above the bed, hanging fixtures such as chandeliers, hanging lamps, air conditioning units, bookshelf racks, or wall cabinets directly above the bed is not advisable from the perspective of Feng Shui internal landform. The fixtures represent an oppressive force that may lead to health problems, psychological problems, or mental health problems for the occupants.

Often, the size of a fixture determines the extent of the problems it poses to the occupant. For example, if the object is just a small lamp bulb, it's not mandatory to remove it as it doesn't pose much of an oppressive issue. An excellent practice and precaution are to remove all hanging structures from above the bed.

If it is essential to keep the fixture in its original position, consider moving the bed, so it does not rest on top of it. However, as bed position is crucial for bedroom Feng Shui landform perspective, ensure it doesn't cause any other landform issues if moved.

Undesirable structural beam and hanging lamps directly above bed

Technique #55 - Underground Basement Bedroom

Most apartments' bedrooms are located on the main or upper floor level as it is preferable for bedroom space accessible with natural sunlight and a window view of the outside environment. Despite this preference, there is an increasing trend of houses getting part of their basement area converted into bedroom uses due to space constraint problems.

However, converting a basement area into bedroom usage may not be recommended from Feng Shui's perspective. Having adequate sunlight at illuminating the room and having positive Chi energy flow is always the topmost concern. If the underground space has no natural sunlight resulting in a stuffy and dark area, it is not advisable to use it for bedroom purposes. This room can be converted into a storage space used for keeping unused items.

Essentially, even if the room does receive a small amount of sunlight from above and is constantly illuminated with a bedroom lamp, it still may not fit the bill of a suitable living bedroom. Because the available living space of an underground area may possess too much negative energy vibe lingering underneath the main level. As a general rule of thumb, avoid using this space for bedroom purposes if there are other suitable rooms at disposal.

Avoid staying in a windowless bedroom in the basement of a house

Technique #56 - Bed Above Kitchen Stove

Many common beliefs regarding the position of the bedroom are that it should not be located directly above the kitchen space, as the strong presence of the Fire element in the kitchen area can adversely affect the Chi energy vibe of the bedroom. This is not an entirely accurate practice because, from the Feng Shui arrangement perspective, we are concerned with the focal structure of each sector instead of the entire compound.

The focal structure of the bedroom is, straightforwardly, the bed. Therefore when considering the bedroom layout, the placement of that bed should never be located directly above the kitchen stove, instead of the whole kitchen. It is never about an overall area but the focal structure of each sector that matters.

In a negative arrangement of the bed above the kitchen stove layout, occupants are likely to suffer constant migraines or sleep-related health problems. The severity of such issues is very much related to the degree of kitchen stove usage. If homeowners seldom cook and kitchen space rarely gets into any cooking activity, the effects of such a negative configuration can be negligible and non-existent.

Placing bed directly above the kitchen stove is not recommended

Technique #57 - Plants in Bedroom

Live plants are ideal for relieving mental tension and stressful eye muscles after a long day at work. Therefore, it is common for homeowners to place them in the bedroom to add some fresh oxygen and freshen up the room with some refreshing green.

However, when placing them in the bedroom area, it is essential to note that the number of potted plants should not be excessive, and homeowners should keep the size of each at the height of under a meter at best.

Live plants can convert their surrounding Chi energy from a passive to a vibrant state after some time. When these plants' size gets too excessive and huge, the generated Chi energy can get too strong and vibrant making it unfit for bedroom area uses. Strong and vibrant Chi energy is more suitable for living room and kitchen space where active Yang activities are present.

In essence, having live plants in the bedroom is recommended for its healing effect and a good use for neutralizing negative internal Feng Shui landforms such as Poison Arrow Chi, generated by pointed wall edges or other sharp objects. As long as the number of plants is kept minimal and often trimmed for height and size, they are generally good in the bedroom.

Avoid having excessive live plants in bedroom with overgrown height

Technique #58 - Work Space Separated From Bedroom

There are different beliefs and contradicting understandings regarding the use of the bedroom area for work-related activity. One school of thought advocates against having a workspace set up in the bedroom area as the sight of a working desk can trigger and distract a person's sleep quality. Another school of thought endorsed the benefit of working in the bedroom space, as it is a quiet and serene environment for getting work done efficiently.

In my opinion, homeowners should separate the workspace from the bedroom compound, but not because the placement of a physical desk can affect a person's sleep and rest. The reason is that according to the principles of classical Feng Shui philosophy, work-related activities are categorized as actions that don't bode well in a bedroom compound.

Feng Shui principles also advocate the bedroom sector as a place of passive Yin energy space and should encompass activities of a similar nature. Job-related working is a type of active Yang activity that is not suitable within the bedroom area. In contrast, activities such as book reading, sleeping, or resting are ideal as they are considered passive Yin activities.

Therefore, if the workspace is incorporated in the bedroom area, occupants may experience difficulties and challenges at their job aspect, resulting in poor work performance over time. A workspace should ideally be situated in an individual workroom separated from other house sectors.

A workspace setup within the bedroom area is not recommended

Chapter 5:
Feng Shui Techniques for Home Office

With the COVID 19 pandemic outbreak across the world in 2019, we have noticed a changing trend of how working employees are no longer required to report to the office to get work completed. Instead, they can simply log in from their work desktop in the comfort of their own home and clock in assigned work as per usual.

Meetings are no longer confined to a conventional meeting room space but are a dial away for online meetings with colleagues dressed down comfortably in their home clothes. This Work-From-Home setup has increased corporate companies' efficiency and cost savings, with many ditching big and expensive office space for a smaller office suite.

In my opinion, this new way of working from home will stick around even after the pandemic has passed since it has shown how effective it can be. As employees spend more time working at home as a result of this arrangement, it is extremely important that the home office setup be in harmony with all the positive aspects of Feng Shui Interior Landform design.

While working from home, many people have the option of setting up their preferred workspace. It can be on a dining table, sofa couch, bed, or even coffee table in front of their television. However, it is not advisable to work at these improper places since they are not intended for work-related activities. It is important to be working in a room with a solid desk table, a chair with good support, adequate lighting, and a comfortable temperature.

Therefore, it would be best suited to be situated in a study room or an additional room dedicated to work. The following pointers are based on a study room or a work-room environment in the house.

Technique #59 - Work Desk and Room Door

When it comes to Feng Shui internal landform configuration for a home office, the facing of a work desk to the room door carries huge significance. It is not advisable for a stationary work desk to be located directly in front of a room door, as the incoming Chi energy flow may collide head-on with the work desk, producing unwanted negative Chi energy. It is acceptable for the work desk to face the room door in a diagonal line of sight, so long as it is not straight-up with the room door.

A work desk's seat should also avoid back-facing the room door for the same reason. The forceful and negative Sha Chi (Killing Energy) caused by this configuration can adversely affect a person's quality of work, relationship with colleagues and superiors, and a general lack of support. To resolve such a problem, place a room divider in the middle to prevent the presence of negative Chi energy from affecting the occupants on the working chair.

Not advisable for work desk to directly face bedroom door entrance

Technique #60 -
Structural Beams Over Work Desk

Structural beams remained a hazardous structure throughout the house premise when people gathered underneath them. Especially for those working at home, be sure that these beams are not directly above the head as their oppressive nature creates suppressing Chi energy that can cause intense stress and pressure when working underneath it. In such circumstances, the most immediate remedy action is moving the work desk away from the beams to avoid any negative Chi energy from affecting personal lifestyle and work.

If there is no better space for relocating the work desk, one solution is to hang two Feng Shui flutes with red strings attached to both ends of the beam structure. Feng Shui flutes are auspicious items capable of neutralizing and negating suppressive and negative Chi energy generated from the ceiling beams.

Avoid having structural beams directly above home office workspace

Technique #61 -
Bright and Illuminated Home Office

In general, residential apartments should keep their interiors bright with sufficient natural lighting or fluorescent lighting. Dim or dark lighting in an apartment home brings about passive Yin energy that is generally undesirable for homeowners. However, not all space within a house requires the same amount of bright lighting.

Bedroom, bathroom, storage room are passive Yin spaces that don't require bright lighting. In contrast, the kitchen, living room, and home office sectors belong to the active Yang energy sector, which requires natural, illuminating sunlight or a strong, bright light source to benefit the energy within. A charged-up, positive, and energized active Yang energy home office can create an uplifting spirit at producing exceptional results at work.

A dark and dimly lighted home office can psychologically affect a person's working mood. It may cause the occupant to feel sleepy, unmotivated, and uninspired to perform at his best in his work duty.

An ideal home office with plenty of natural sunlight

Technique #62 -
Shape of Home Office Room

The shape of the home office room is best suited to a square or rectangular shape layout. Similar to the principle of work desk shape, these balanced layouts allow Chi energy to flow evenly. As square or rectangular rooms are symmetrical in shape, they usually do not possess problems of a missing sector.

A house with missing sectors denotes the inability to harness Chi energy in the home associated with that direction and location. This is an unfavorable configuration according to advanced methodologies like Xuan Kong Flying Star and Eight Mansions method to ascertain the orientation and strength of Chi flow.

Another plus point for a square or rectangular shape layout is the absence of Poison Arrow Chi within the room, which can create work and health problems for occupants. An L-Shape room layout possesses a 90-degree sharp edge wall located in the middle where the two walls meet, creating unwanted negative Sha Chi (Killing Energy) within the room.

Recommended square shape home office room layout for balanced Chi distribution

Technique #63 - Avoid Windowless Room

When choosing the home office location, be sure to pick one that has a good natural flow of air in and out of the room. By that, it often requires the presence of windows on the side of the room for air ventilation and circulation. A well-ventilated room often helps Chi energy flow better and prevents the presence of stagnant Chi residing in dead corners of the room.

Do also make sure to leave the windows open whenever possible. Because the circulation of Chi energy happens only when existing Chi in the room is able to get out efficiently before new incoming Chi energy can replace them. Therefore, having closed windows in the home-office room is very similar to a windowless room, which is bad for the circulation of Chi energy in a confined space.

It is generally not recommended for a home office to reside in the basement area of a house as it usually lacks spacious windows for a proper circulation flow of Chi energy to take place. However, its not a sweeping generalisation for all basement orientations. Do consult with a trained practitioner to ascertain the suitability of the basement compound if need be.

Avoid using windowless room as home office in basement of an apartment

Technique #64 -
Seating with Good Support

For office Feng Shui analysis, the location of the seat is vital in determining the relationship with colleagues and superiors, work performance, and even the stability of the job position. From the home-office setup, the emphasis is equally important on the working chair, and it is highly advisable for the back of the chair to face the wall.

Under more comprehensive scrutiny, it is highly preferred if the chair has a high back for its resounding support. It will also be most efficient to have a brick wall instead of a partial partition wall made with sheer quality often found in makeshift apartment rooms, used as a backing for the chair.

Great emphasis is placed on the back of the seating position because it represents job stability and the support of Noblemen (贵人) in the work environment. Employees frequently experience unhealthy relationships with their managers by being threatened with being fired from their jobs. Poor seating arrangements can likely cause this without proper wall support at their working spot.

High back office chair with back facing sturdy wall for support in work environment

Technique #65 - Poison Arrow Chi in Home Office

By this chapter, most readers should have been familiar with the impact of Poison Arrow Chi in an apartment. To reiterate, these are forceful and negative Sha Chi (Killing Energy) that points sharply towards an important structure of the apartment. It's generally created by sharp edges of walls or furniture with pointy corners.

It's essential to make sure that the Poison Arrow Chi doesn't have its sharp edges facing the home office door to ensure that the state of Chi energy remains excellent and positive within the room. Another consideration is to ensure the work desk is unaffected by this negative formation. Having one in these two areas can negatively affect work promotion and induce chances of accidents at home.

Eliminate and neutralize these negative Sha Chi by smothering the sharp edges of the wall or pointy corners. Alternatively, place some vine leaves or potted plants to cover them up so no sharp edges can be seen.

Avoid having Poison Arrow Chi from sharp wall edges pointing towards work desk direction

Technique #66 - Celestial Animal Work Area Formation

According to classical Feng Shui studies, the formation of the four celestial mythical animals (Green Dragon, White Tiger, Black Turtle, Red Phoenix) determines every house's flow of Chi energy externally. Every legendary animal represents a specific direction, color, element, and purpose. In Feng Shui internal landform context, we are interested in the combinational use of the Green Dragon position and White Tiger position when interpolated in the work area setup. When a work area is correctly purposed in these formations, the occupant can benefit from good career progression with an abundance of promotions and salary increment opportunities.

The Green Dragon position represents the left side of the entire work area (as viewed from the seating position). It's an auspicious direction that symbolizes wealth, power, and authority in the formation. To receive the associated benefits, the Green Dragon position of the work area must be activated with the correct placement of items. The use of books, journals, publications, work-related manuals that represent knowledge and wisdom can be placed here. These are categorized as positive items that suit the Green Dragon position.

The White Tiger position represents the right side of the work area (as viewed from the seating position). It is considered an inauspicious direction that symbolizes problems, vexation, and hiccups at work. With the placement of electronic devices like computers, printers, fax machines, mobile phones, etc., the White Tiger position can be deactivated in the workplace, neutralizing such problems. Electronic items symbolize a type of disturbance and a source of negative energy from **Feng Shui** philosophy. Therefore it suits the negative nature of the White Tiger position.

The White Tiger position and Green Dragon position of a working area setup

Technique #67 - Spacious Area Infront Work Desk

When an empty and spacious area is situated right in front of the work desk, a small Bright Hall (名堂) area is considered present in the working environment. It is an auspicious Feng Shui internal landform since it contains Chi energy by circling it, preventing it from escaping, and keeping it focused in the area. The positive Chi energy will linger longer in the working space, allowing those at work to perform better in their job.

Those who work from home usually have an easier time setting up Bright Hall configurations in their apartment than in their office complex. Other than a boss or higher management staff, office employees are generally not provided with additional space for personal use other than their standard working desk or cubicle. Therefore homeowners can tailor the size of their Bright Hall area to preferences if the office is located at home.

Although having a bigger Bright Hall is better as you can facilitate a greater amount of Chi energy flow, having a good balance is the key criteria to maintaining an auspicious internal Feng Shui configuration. Therefore the size of the Bright Hall area should always be in good ratio to the size of the room.

Recommended for big and spacious area in front of home office work desk

Technique #68 - Avoid Back Facing Window

From Feng Shui principles, the best seating arrangement has the working chair back facing a solid wall in the room as this offers the best support for career progression.

As a practical matter, however, households in land-scarce countries, such as Singapore and Hong Kong, are generally smaller and have limited room for furniture arrangements. When faced with a packed room full of furniture and living necessities, some may not have the option of choosing this type of configuration layout for their working seat arrangement.

In such circumstances, some work desks may end up having their seating position back facing a window panel. This is not a recommended Feng Shui internal landform as the window opening resembles a broken hole in the wall facade that denotes poor support and deteriorating performance in work. One quick remedy is to install a thick and good-quality curtain to cover up the window opening entirely.

Avoid positioning the home office chair back facing the window panel

Technique #69 - Shape of Work Desk

New age furniture comes with an assortment of contemporary designs that may challenge the traditional design norm. Working desks sometimes feature quirky and creative designs intended more to generate a viral buzz on social media than to provide any functional purpose. Even common L-shape long desks are not suitable for work usage as they are considered to be odd shapes.

In Feng Shui studies, it is recommended to adopt ordinary shapes such as square or rectangular work desks instead of quirky and odd shape designs. It is because these balanced shapes work desks are terrific at creating an equilibrium of passive Yin and active Yang energy around the area. Besides, the four corners of the balanced shapes work desk help to channel incoming Chi energy to flow in a balanced manner around the room, ultimately increasing positive Chi flow.

L shape work desk with creative design not suitable for work usage

Chapter 6:
Feng Shui Techniques for Door

As a Feng Shui practitioner, identifying the Chi energy strength within a property or workplace is the most critical factor in determining its quality for staying or business uses. This is the focus of every Feng Shui consultation where the external environment and interior configuration are thoroughly examined to determine what level of Chi energy is residing within the premise.

The use of the main door is significant in Feng Shui philosophy as it is known as the "Chi mouth" of a residence, where external environment Chi energy enters the house and interacts with occupants. When positive Feng Shui landforms surround the main door, it can capture positive Chi energy essence and distribute the benefits to the entire household. The reverse is true when the main entrance is situated around negative Feng Shui landforms. It negatively influences and affects people with problems and hindrances in life.

In this chapter, we will be looking at both the internal and external environment of a house main entrance in search of Feng Shui landform that can either enhance or decrease the receptivity of Chi energy flow. In simple terms, the external environment is the house's outdoor area, while the internal environment is the inside of the house viewed from the door's position.

Technique #70 - Size of Main Door

The size of the main door should always be the biggest door in the entire house. Due to the fact that the entrance is the Chi mouth of the premises, big entrances can readily gather and invite more Chi energy from the surrounding environment into the house, thereby increasing the strength of Chi energy within.

It has always been advocated that a homeowner's goal should be to fill their house with an endless amount of good Chi energy, which they can use to create a positive environment. However, do take note that it's not always the case where the bigger the entrance is, the more affluent and prosperous the family will be. Because if this were the case, everyone would have built a two-story door big enough for a giant to pass through, wouldn't they? Keeping the size of the main entrance proportional to that of the property is of the utmost importance over here.

Ideally, the rest of the doors within the property should be the same size, while the main entrance should remain the biggest. Suppose there are other doors that are bigger than the main entrance. In that case, Chi's equilibrium is unsettled, and it can easily create an imbalance of Chi energy flow within the residential compound.

When the master bedroom door is significantly bigger than the main door, problems with relationships, marriage, and emotional control are sure to develop. Similarly, when the kitchen compound door is bigger than the main entrance, problems related to wealth, career, and business will predominantly surface.

The main door size is disproportionately small for a big house

Technique #71 - The External Bright Hall (External Environment)

The Bright Hall was the designated space in the Royal Palace where Emperors and their advisors met to discuss politics and governance. This area is reserved mainly for important issues and events because it is a thriving area with the most Chi energy flowing.

In today's time, the Bright Hall refers to a spacious, bright, clean, and empty area primarily used to gather surrounding Chi energy. When the front of the main entrance is adorned with such an area, the collected Chi energy can easily flow into the house, filling it with abundant positive Chi energy.

When setting up the Bright Hall outside of the house front door, it is recommended to build some minor fencing around the area. The fenced-up perimeter gives the porous area a defined space for Chi to collect and settle in. This way, Chi energy can gather in this area without dissipating away quickly.

Large and spacious Bright Hall area outside main entrance with semi-enclosed perimeter is an ideal layout

Technique #72 - Long Winding Road Formation (External Environment)

The external environment outside the door must be given considerable attention while evaluating the Feng Shui landform for the main door.

Standing from the main door position and looking out of the house, if a stretch of long winding road leads out from the door, it is an undesirable Long Winding Road Formation (直冲煞) that should be avoided at all costs. Like a long sword 'piercing' the house entrance, this negative landform creates strong and negative Sha Chi (Killing Energy) that can affect family members with chronic disease and illness, loss of wealth, and even accidents.

One way to circumvent this problem is to change the position of the main door. Move it a few meters to either side so that it is not directly facing the entrance of the long winding road. Once the position is changed, the adverse effects it has on the family members are negligible. However, if changing the door position is simply out of the question, check out if there are any structures or objects found between the path. The sight of bushes or potted plants between the door and road can block out some or most of the negative Sha Chi energy.

Long Winding Road outside of a house main entrance is inauspicious

Technique #73 - Reverse Bow Formation (External Environment)

In many high-rise property houses in the city area, a common negative landform is the Reverse Bow Formation (反弓煞) typically caused by the interwinding nature of expressways or highway roads. When a road is bent or constructed circularly, a curvature on the exterior form is formed. This curvature generates waves of strong and forceful negative Sha Chi (Killing Energy) that are undesirable for the house when facing the main entrance.

This formation resembles a sickle knife that is slicing up whatever lies ahead of its path. The longer or wider the curvature is, the stronger the adverse effect it has on the family household. This negative landform should be highly avoided as it may cause accidents, wealth problems, and sickness to the homeowners.

One remedy to such landform is to plant some trees in front of the main door area. These trees can block out and neutralize the effects of these forceful negative Sha Chi energy. Alternatively, occupants may consider changing the direction of the door so that it is not directly facing the Reverse Bow Formation.

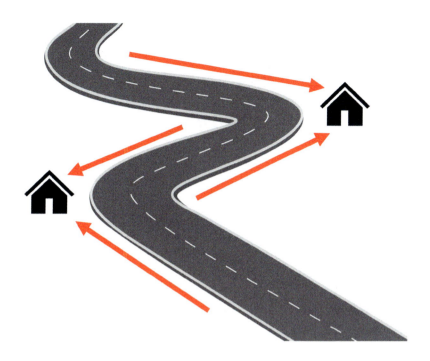

Avoid having a reverse bow formation facing the house's main entrance

Technique #74 - Sharp Sha Formation (External Environment)

Sharp Sha Formation (尖角煞) is created by buildings, objects, or structures with sharp exteriors that emit forceful and negative Sha Chi (Killing Energy). This is similar to Poison Arrow Chi because both are caused by sharp angles. Although they are commonly found in a house's internal and external landscape, the adverse effect of the Sharp Sha Formation is huge and should be avoided as much as possible.

If Sharp Sha Formation directly faces the house's front door, it can cause financial loss, disharmony relationship, sickness within the family and should be avoided as far as possible. However, even if it is so, do not get all alarmed and start planning on moving out of the home, as several considerations can change the severity of such a negative landform. If the horizontal distance between the sharp structure and the house is far apart, the impact can be negligible and need not be taken seriously.

In addition, when the pointy structure is not on the same level and has a huge height disparity with the main door, its adverse effects are significantly reduced. For example, suppose the housing unit is on the fifteenth floor, and opposite the main entrance is a three-story building with a sharp roof. In that case, the negative Sha Chi energy affecting the residence is inconsequential due to the vast difference in a vertical level.

Avoid Sharp Sha Formation created by a sharp edge on the exterior of a building facing the house front door

Technique #75 - T-Junction Formation (External Environment)

The T-Junction Formation (丁字煞) is considered a negative Feng Shui formation. It can hinder a homeowner's career and cause health issues if it sits near their house. Not to be confused with the Long Winding Road Formation, T-Junction Formation has two stretches of road in contact at right angles, forming up the letter 'T'. In fact, T-Junction Formation is the deadlier formation of two due to a higher degree of negative Sha Chi (Killing Energy) contributed by the additional road.

What is the way to identify a house if it is affected by this landform? Observing from the house's main entrance, if the line of sight falls within the width of the road and is in front of the center of the intersection, the apartment is unfortunately afflicted by a T-Junction Formation.

Unlike most Feng Shui consultants advocating a change of house or major renovation work to counteract such negative landform, the actual impact needs to be carefully analyzed before taking any drastic circumventing measures. The amount of traffic flowing within the roads is one key consideration factor. Suppose the T-Junction is located in a relatively rural area with few cars and traffic. In that case, the associated problem with such landform is small as the negative Sha Chi energy generated is negligible. This therefore requires no major alteration other than introducing some trees or bushes near the main door compound to block out any residual negative Sha Chi energy.

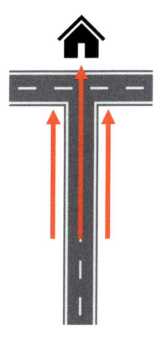

Avoid T-Junction Formation caused by house main entrance facing intersection of two road facing the house front door

Technique #76 - Knife in Sky Formation (External Environment)

When two buildings closely situated to each other exist a narrow space gap between them, it is known as Knife in Sky Formation (天斩煞). This negative landform creates a huge amount of forceful and negative Sha Chi (Killing Energy) when it is seen directly opposite the house's main entrance. The narrower the distance between two buildings, the more it resembles a sharp knife ready to slice up the residence from the opposite.

However, if the two buildings are situated far from the residence, negative Sha Chi energy impacting the house is relatively small and can be disregarded. The actual distance is not a fixed number because multiple variables like the height of the apartment and the size of the space gap can affect the seriousness of such formation. The general rule of thumb is if it is located one kilometer away, it has no severe impact on homeowners.

In addition, for high-rise apartments affected by such formation, the opposite buildings have to be of equal height or higher to be of valid threat. If the buildings with Knife in Sky Formation are just a mere ten-story high while the homeowners live on the 25th floor, the housing unit is not fully exposed to the negative Sha Chi forces.

Avoid staying in apartments that have front door facing Knife in Sky Formation

Technique #77 - Main Entrance Facing Slope (External Environment)

From a Feng Shui standpoint, a sloping pathway or driveway outside the main entrance is not a recommended landform. Because a downward slope possesses a natural gravitational pulling force that rapidly causes Chi energy to flow out of the main door compound. This is an undesirable effect because a household can only be prosperous and wealthy when the front door compound is able to collect and hold on to the surrounding Chi energy effectively. A rapid flow out of Chi energy can render the residence with inadequate Chi energy resulting in loss of wealth, poor health, or hindrance in career advancement for family members.

On the contrary, if the slope outside the main entrance is upward angled, it can be a positive landform. Similar to the gravitational pulling theory, Chi energy is now flowing towards the direction of the main door from a higher elevated level. This means a greater amount of Chi energy congregates in the front door compound, which is a good sign from Feng Shui's philosophy.

However, the determining factor as to whether an upward slope is considered a positive or negative landform relies on the slope's gradient. A highly acute upward angled slope can cause strong and forceful Chi energy to flow downwards to the main door entrance. This energy subsequently becomes negative Sha Chi (Killing Energy) that is unsuitable for the house premise. The 'perfect slope' is one that is gently upwards angled, delivering slow and positive Chi energy down towards the main entrance.

Inauspicious for main house entrance facing downward slope driveway

Technique #78 - Bright, Clean and Uncluttered Entrance (External Environment)

A simple way of maintaining the front entrance in an ideal Feng Shui environment is ensuring the front door area is kept in a bright, clean, and clutter-free state at all times. Ensuring these three requirements are met in the main entry area helps ensure that Chi energy in that space remains good and maximizes the potential for gathering positive Chi energy.

From a psychological perspective, keeping the main entrance neat and pleasing to the eye by maintaining these conditions is one way of strengthening the mental health of homeowners. Imagine returning home, and the first sight is greeted by a dark, dirty, and messy door entrance. What sort of vibes are created in association with the homecoming? Not a good one, I suppose! Switch for a change in the environment and observe the positive change it can have in your life.

A bright, clean and uncluttered front entrance is highly recommended

Technique #79 - Pillar Structure at Main Entrance (External Environment)

The best orientation for any main entrance is to have a spacious, empty, bright, and uncluttered area at the front allowing Chi energy to gather and flow into the apartment. When an erected pillar or lamppost structure is in front of the main entrance, it obstructs the flow of Chi energy by disrupting the environment conducive to its clustering and collecting. Therefore, a negative landform like this shouldn't appear outside of an apartment's main door.

When faced with such a negative landform, homeowners do not always have an easy solution for rectification. Because pillars are the structural design of an apartment that can't be removed or switched of position easily without spending tons of money on renovation works. And that can only be considered a viable option if the pillar structure is an asset of homeowners in the first place. It will be out of the question if a public property like a lamppost falls outside of a personal land-use area.

Under such circumstances, the solution may not be restricted to devising remedy action to improve the Chi energy flow. The recommended remedy is to open up another door in the premises and start using that as the main entrance instead. This is a much easier and cheaper option than altering the façade of the pillar or the main entrance.

It is important to note that such negative landform is not restricted to pillar structures, but any structural designs that resemble one, such as a lamppost, traffic light, billboards, etc.

Avoid staying in apartments that have lamppost structure in front of house main entrance

Technique #80 - Door Facing Dead-End Road (External Environment)

Some homeowners love the idea of having their houses in front of a cul-de-sac road as they are typically more quiet, serene and generate a lesser amount of traffic noises from this type of dead-end street. However, these are as far as the benefits of such a residence go as it is not ideal to have such a road located near the main door entrance.

This is because a dead-end street is a common culmination spot for negative Si Chi 死气 (Dead Energy) as Chi energy flow gets blocked easily when one end of the exit is closed off. This is akin to a clogged drainage system where the choked stagnant water turns foul after a prolonged period. When the main residence entrance is near, it collects negative Chi energy from the road and distributes it back to the house premises. Therefore it is advisable for a house to be near an open-ended road instead of a closed-end street where the front door entrance is.

Not recommended for houses to be in front of a cul-de-sac road

Technique #81 - Door-Facing-Door Formation (External Environment)

A Door-Facing-Door Formation is a common sight in high-rise apartment homes where the main entrance of one unit faces the entrance to another unit. According to the seating and facing position of the occupant's house, the main entrance either acts as a Chi energy's entry or exit outlet. In either case, the Door-Facing-Door Formation is not ideal for the main entrance compound.

As a front porch is used as the entryway for Chi energy into the house, the door from another unit provides an opening for it to escape, causing energy flow to be weak and irregular around the main entryway compound. Alternatively, the main entrance of the house can also be the exit portal for Chi energy. This causes unwanted turbulence of energy vibe to develop around the main door compound when Chi energy leaves the compound and gets sucked in by the opposite door.

The mitigating factor for such negative formation is to analyze the distance between both doors. When the gap is wide and apart, negative effects are substantially reduced. Remedy actions can be changing the position or tilting the direction of the entrance to the point that it isn't facing the opposite door head-on.

Door-Facing-Door Formation caused by two front door facing each other in close proximity

Technique #82 -
Door Facing Lift (External Environment)

Many homeowners prefer to have a lift facility close to their house unit in high-rise apartment buildings as it increases accessibility for their daily usage. However, it is important to note that the lift structure shall never be directly in front of the main entrance. This type of negative layout is common in some land-constrained housing projects where common corridor space is limited.

Lift is a vertical moving structure that stimulates the environmental Chi energy constantly. Due to this, the Chi energy surrounding the main entrance is constantly in a state of unrest when the lift is situated on the opposite side. In Feng Shui studies of Chi energy flow, this is unfavorable because positive energy should be calm, composed, and slow-moving.

Some bungalows or semi-detached houses have an internal lift system. Is that considered a bad Feng Shui landform by having it within the house compound? The answer is, it depends on the frequency of lift usage within the household. The use of a lift in a high-rise apartment building is undoubtedly high as the entire block of residents commonly shares it. Therefore it can be considered a straight-up negative landform. In comparison, lift's usage for one family household in a single house can be limited. Thus, the associated problem with having such a facility can be negligible.

Not advisable for the house front entrance to directly face the lift opening

Technique #83 - Door Facing Staircase (External Environment)

Modern residential high-rise buildings rarely utilize the staircase. This is because the staircase mainly serves an auxiliary function, for example, during fire emergencies or when the lift malfunctions. Therefore they are usually positioned at the far end of a corridor level in an apartment building due to such low usage. However, some older residential apartment buildings still use staircases as their primary facility due to the lack of a working lift. It's a common sight to have a staircase landing directly in front of some older housing units.

This is a negative landform from Feng Shui philosophy as the constant movement around the main door area exuberates surrounding Chi energy to an irregular and vibrating state. This is a similar concept to having a lift facility in front of the main entrance, so the mitigating factor of such landform remains the same.

If the staircase is seldom used, adverse effects on the housing unit are not widespread and often can be disregarded. In retrospect, a high footfall staircase can trigger problems related to holding and preserving wealth, financial hardship, and career stagnation for household members.

Older housing unit has its front door facing staircase landings that are considered inauspicious

Technique #84 -
Door Facing Exit (Internal Environment)

Standing from the house main door position and looking within, the direct line-of-sight shouldn't reside a window, balcony, or a backdoor, as it resembles an exit outlet of Chi. It is a bad Feng Shui layout as Chi energy gets exited from the house almost immediately after entering the main entrance.

For a property to be prosperous, the layout design must allow Chi energy to slowly circulate in the residential compound before making its way out naturally. Door Facing Exit arrangement forces Chi energy out of the house in a rush manner and doesn't allow it to stay long enough to impact the family household positively. This can result in family members having constant problems in relation to money and may eventually find themselves in financial hardship.

However, contrary to most Feng Shui consultants advice, not all negative layouts like this need a remedy. First, we need to determine the severity of the problem stemming from such a negative arrangement. If the distance between the door and exit is relatively wide and apart, meaning in between may lie a living room space, or a dining area adorned with numerous big pieces of furniture, Chi energy doesn't have a straight-through exit route out of the house. Therefore, the severity of such a bad interior landform is not huge and can be negligible.

We may also compare the size of the exit to the main entrance to determine the extent of the problem. For example, suppose the exit outlet is a single-window panel at the back while the main entrance is a huge double slab door commonly found in larger residences. In that case, the entering Chi energy is far larger than those exiting. Hence, the severity of such a layout is minuscular and needs no rectification action.

Opening the front door to a direct sight of the window panel is not an ideal configuration

Technique #85 - The Internal Bright Hall (Internal Environment)

After understanding the importance of having an external Bright Hall area at the main door entrance, having a similar layout in the internal portion of the front entrance can be highly advantageous as well. An internal Bright Hall area right before the main door attracts and retains the surrounding Chi energy before circulating them to the rest of the house.

The Bright Hall works like a pump that delivers positive Chi energy to different house areas, similar to a heart organ that pumps essential oxygenated blood to the rest of body parts. Without this area, positive Chi energy entering from the main door might not reach different parts of the house efficiently.

Therefore a clean, bright, clutter-free Bright Hall area can extend the positive energy to the rest of the premise with ease.

Highly recommended for a spacious Bright Hall area in the internal portion of the house front entrance

Technique #86 -
Door Facing Wall (Internal Environment)

When a wall is located in close proximity to the main door entrance, the flow of Chi energy from the external area into the house is affected. An erected wall takes away the necessary space for Chi energy to gather and circulate at the immediate front portion of the main door. In **Feng Shui** studies, it is a negative interior configuration to avoid during the construction and renovation phase of the apartment.

From a psychological viewpoint, to be confronted by a wall upon entering one's house would have been distressing. In comparison, facing a spacious, bright, and uncluttered area at the front portion of the main door will give off a better vibe for family members and visitors entering the house.

Houses with this type of negative layout can arise to limited wealth-making opportunities, hindrance in career progression, and various health ailments for homeowners.

House front door facing too close to an internal wall is an undesirable layout

Technique #87 -
Door Facing Mirror (Internal Environment)

Mirrors are often placed in the living room area to visually expand the living space to look more spacious than it is. Homeowners also install them for aesthetic purposes or simply for practical uses, like getting a final check on the outfit before leaving home. Often, the main door entrance is in the reflected angle of the mirror when the living room is next to the door.

From the study of Feng Shui philosophy, mirrors can reflect and vibrate the surrounding energy due to their reflecting nature. When the main door entrance faces a mirror surface, Chi energy flowing into the house premises gets unnecessarily vibrated. Chi energy is most desirable and auspicious when its calm and slow-moving state. Therefore such vibrancy caused by mirrors is to be avoided as far as possible.

Front door directly facing mirror at entrance is not recommended

About The Author

Dominique Cai

Dominique came from a strong lineage of geomancy masters, and Feng Shui thought leaders. Currently the second generation of Feng Shui consultants, he inherited more than 40 years of wisdom, experience, and knowledge in metaphysics and ancient geomancy.

Before taking over the business, Dominique had a successful career in the banking industry, helping High-Net-Worth clients strategize, plan, and achieve their investment goals.

An entrepreneur with a passion for helping everyday people gain financial freedom and protect themselves against economic crisis, he quit his stellar banking career to start a precious metals company. The company's mission is to provide investment-grade bullions to help average citizens protect wealth by converting liquid assets to hard commodities.

Six months after the company's incorporation, it reached the monumental milestone of $1 million in revenue, breaking the industry's norm. He is often labeled as the industry changer for introducing several schemes to provide affordable precious metal ownership to the general public.

With an eventual plan to continue the family heritage, he cashed out on his successful business and returned to his roots of helping people from all walks of life prosper and thrive using time-tested metaphysical strategies.

Dominique was a Certified Financial Consultant and held various licenses for finance-related activities in Singapore. His vast experience and knowledge in the finance and investment sector have greatly helped him gel ancient metaphysical strategies that worked well in modern and current times.

Currently the Chief Executive of regional Feng Shui powerhouse Nine Wealth Palace (ninewp.com), he resides in Singapore. He is a Master Trainer for a wide range of metaphysical studies and Lead Consultant for domestic and international clients specializing in residential, corporate, and government-linked projects.

Printed in Great Britain
by Amazon

79472666R00119